Physical Characterist

King Charles Sp

(from The Kennel Club bree

Body: Chest wide and deep, back short and level.

Colour: Tricolour: ground pearly white, with well distributed black patches, brilliant tan markings on cheeks, linings of ears, under tail and spots over eyes. Wide white blaze between eyes and up forehead.

Tail: Well feathered, not carried over or above level of back. Docking optional.

Hindquarters: Sufficient muscle to give positive driving movement, stifles well bent, hocks well let down and defined. Straight when viewed from behind, turning neither in nor out.

Size: Weight: 3.6–6.3 kgs (8–14 lbs).

Feet: Compact, well padded and feathered, toes well knuckled, round cat-shaped foot, well cushioned.

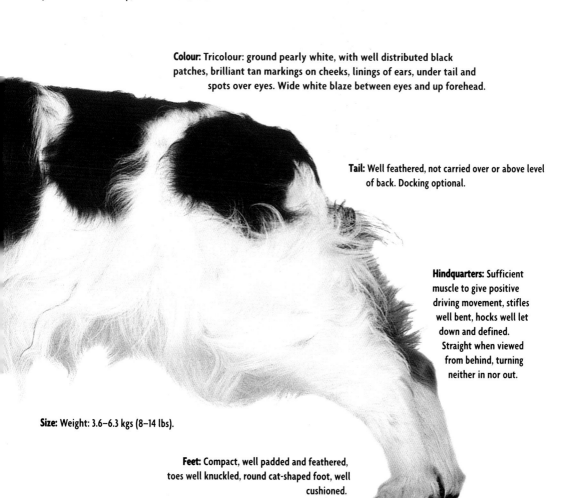

King Charles Spaniel

By Lee Sherwin

Contents

Health Care of Your King Charles Spaniel   **97**

Discover how to select a proper veterinary surgeon and care for your dog at all stages of life. Topics include vaccinations, skin problems, dealing with external and internal parasites and common medical and behavioural conditions.

Your Veteran King Charles Spaniel   **127**

Consider the care of your veteran King Charles Spaniel, including the proper diet for a veteran. Recognise the signs of an ageing dog, both behavioural and medical; implement a special-care programme with your veterinary surgeon and become comfortable with making the final decisions and arrangements for your senior King Charles Spaniel.

Showing Your King Charles Spaniel   **135**

Experience the conformation dog show world. Learn about The Kennel Club, the different types of shows and the making up of a champion. Also learn about the FCI, the world's international kennel club.

Behaviour of Your King Charles Spaniel   **145**

Learn to recognise and handle common behavioural problems in your King Charles Spaniel. Topics discussed include separation anxiety, jumping up, barking, chewing, digging, begging, etc.

Photography by Carol Ann Johnson with additional photographs by:

Norvia Behling, TJ Calhoun, Carolina Biological Supply, David Dalton, Doskocil, Isabelle Français, James Hayden-Yoav, James R Hayden, RBP, Bill Jonas, Dwight R Kuhn, Dr Dennis Kunkel, Mikki Pet Products, Phototake, Jean Claude Revy, Dr Andrew Spielman and Alice van Kempen.

The publisher would like to thank all of the owners of the dogs featured in this book, including Mea Askins, Jussi Palosaari and Eugene Zaphiris.

PUBLISHED IN THE UNITED KINGDOM BY:

INTERPET
PUBLISHING

Vincent Lane, Dorking, Surrey RH4 3YX England

ISBN 1-84286-029-1

The regal King Charles Spaniel is a true combination of beauty, dignity and personality. Known as a toy dog throughout the world, this diminutive spaniel with an aristocratic past is a popular and charming companion.

A toy dog through and through, the King Charles Spaniel is classified in the Toy Group of breeds in the UK and on the Continent as well as in the US and Canada. In North America, however, he is known as the English Toy Spaniel. Whatever his name, this is a delightful toy spaniel from England to whom we will refer in this book as the King Charles Spaniel.

Working dogs have been around for centuries, bred to assist humans with various jobs and chores. The pastoral dogs would herd and guard the sheep and cattle, and the hounds coursed after deer, rabbits or whatever could be put upon man's table for a meal. The terriers, large and small, evolved into fast, spirited dogs who could rid a farm of foxes, woodchucks and badgers and who could rid an home of rodents and vermin. The gundogs evolved early on to assist the hunter in bringing home his quarry for the family's table. All of these dogs had a purpose and were bred to make humans' lives easier. The dogs that were unable to do the job for which they were bred were disposed of, and those

An early illustration of 'Blenheim Spaniels.' Bred and kept by the Duke of Marlborough, the chestnut and white variety was named for his family's place of residence, Blenheim Palace.

OUR BREED'S NAMESAKE
The interests of King Charles II included the theatre, gambling and horseracing. His court was worldly and extravagant, and there was no secret about his many mistresses nor the rumoured 17 children that he had by them.

who could do a good day's work were bred.

Over the generations, talents and abilities were honed and perfected: the dogs became keener of eyesight and scent, swifter of leg and quicker at the hunt. These were the dogs that lived and worked side by side with man, becoming part of his work force but not always members of his family.

Toy dogs have been around for centuries as well, belonging to the aristocrats and the royalty, whether in England, France, China or Egypt. Dr Johannes Caius wrote in *Of English Dogs*, written in Latin in 1536, 'These dogs are little, pretty and fine, and sought for to satisfy the delicateness of dainty dames and wanton women's wills, instruments of folly for them to play and dally with, to trifle away the treasure of time. These puppies, the smaller

Champions of the 1930s, left to right: Ch Ashton-More Domino, Ch Cystal, Ch Ashton-More Crusader, Ch Ashton-More Wildflower and Ch Barritone.

From the early 1930s, this illustration was reproduced from a pastel drawing specially made for *Hutchinson's Dog Encyclopaedia* by the famous animal artist, Mrs G Shaw-Baker. Shown are the Blenheim and Prince Charles varieties of the King Charles Spaniels.

they be, the more pleasure they provoke, as more meet play-fellows for mincing mistresses to bear in their bosoms.'

COMFORTERS AND FLEA TRAPS

The toy dogs were sometimes called 'Comforter' dogs. In the 16th and 17th centuries, bathing was not done on a regular basis and personal hygiene was poor compared to modern standards. Dogs were often held on laps with the thought that the dog would become host to the fleas that were on the mistress or master. These dogs were also referred to as 'living flea traps.' In addition, the dogs were used for warmth in the draughty palaces and manses.

As civilisation advanced, man realised that dogs could be bred for pleasure as well as for work, and, as the Industrial Revolution began to lighten man's work load, he had more of an inclination to bring the dog inside and to make it his companion. For the lofty role of companion dog, it was

Two King Charles Spaniels owned by Mrs A H Bradley were among the participants in the Ladies' Kennel Club show of May 1931, held at Olympia.

Ch Ashton-More Baronet, bred by Mr F G Borryer, was exhibited in the early 20th century and was an important sire.

over 10 pounds, the toys have been referred to by big-dog owners as fops, mutants and neurotics, and their owners were thought to be individuals who only liked to sit around with a dog up the sleeve or on the lap. On the contrary, although most all dogs like to sit on or near their masters or mistresses, toy dogs can be tough little tykes who can stand their ground, take a good

difficult to find a better pet than a toy dog. With the toys, one would have the choice of a smooth or long coat, a long or cobby body, a pushed-in or elongated muzzle and short or long legs. Whatever the toy dog's physical construction, they all have affectionate natures and a longing to be close to their master's or mistress's side.

Because of the diminutive size of these dogs, few weighing much

'TIL DEATH DO US PART

Mary, Queen of Scots was said to have had a small dog hiding in her skirts at the time of her execution. When discovered later, the dog was covered with his mistress's blood.

When Charles I was put to death, a spaniel walked beside him to the place of his execution and the little dog was put on display that night by the soldiers.

Born in 1927, Ch Ashton-More Nebo won his first Challenge Certificate in 1929. He weighed 9.5 pounds and is considered to be exemplary of breed type at that time.

walk through the park or jump the hoops in agility or the hurdles in obedience, just like the big dogs. The toy dog, whether it be the Maltese in his glorious white coat, the Yorkshire Terrier with his steel-grey flowing coat, the King Charles Spaniel with his glorious colours and 'pug' face or any of the other delightful small breeds, all are great pets and highly competitive in the Best in Show ring.

The toy spaniel was originally believed to have come from the

A drawing from around the turn of the 20th century of 'Lord Tennyson,' a noted winner of his time.

Far East, China or Japan. The pushed-in nose and the protruding eyes are reminiscent of the very old Eastern breeds, the Pekingese and the Japanese Chin. Some thought has been given to the possibility of the dog's originally having come from Spain, the home of the 'spaniels,'

THE KING SPEAKS

In 1903, King Charles fanciers tried to change the name of the breed to the Toy Spaniel but King Edward VII, an ardent supporter of the breed, objected to the name change. Thus, the breed in the United Kingdom has remained the King Charles Spaniel.

and then arriving in the East, where eventually it was exported to England via Holland or France. There is a possibility that Captain Saris, a British naval officer, took a pair of dogs back to England with him in the early 1600s as a gift for King James I from the Japanese Emperor, as the Japanese always included dogs with their royal presents.

The history of these wonderful little spaniels has been recorded quite well in England through the work of our nation's superb portraitists, especially Van Dyck's paintings in the 17th century. The dogs often were pictured with both King Charles I and King Charles II, thus their

Some believe that the toy spaniel originated with dogs from the Far East. The face and eyes of the Pekingese, shown here, certainly bear resemblance to those of the King Charles.

The Pug, shown here, was also popular with royalty in the early days of the King Charles Spaniel.

name, the King Charles Spaniel, even though the dog had been known in England since the 1500s. The spaniel remained very popular with the royals through the reign of James II and it was also popular in France during the reign of Henri III. With the fall of the house of Stuart, the King Charles Spaniel lost its place of favour as William and Mary preferred the other popular toy, the Pug.

The original King Charles Spaniels were only black and tan in colour, with the other three colour varieties being developed at later times. Some confusion about the dogs developed over the years because of the different names that were given to the various colour combinations. Although the toy spaniels were all of the same type, different names were given to each classification of coat colour. The original black and tan variety was called King Charles, the solid red coloration was called Ruby, the tricolour pattern was called Prince Charles and the chestnut and white pattern was called Blenheim. These names are still applied to the colours, though all varieties are regarded as King Charles Spaniels and shown in the same classes at shows.

The King Charles Spaniel, although primarily a companion dog, originally was used as a hunting dog, as were all of the

The original King Charles Spaniel was the black and tan; at one time no other colours existed. Thus, the black and tan has retained the name 'King Charles' to designate its colour variety.

other, larger, spaniels. John Churchill, the first Duke of Marlborough, was an avid fancier and used his dogs for hunting woodcocks and other small game birds. The use of these small dogs for hunting waned, as the dogs tired quickly. The larger spaniels took over from the small dogs, as they were able to work a whole day in the field alongside their masters.

The Duke bred the chestnut and white spaniels, thus the name Blenheim, for the family's residence. At Blenheim Palace can be seen a portrait by Sir Godfrey Kneller, picturing the small chestnut and white spaniels at the feet or in the laps of the women. It

FOUR COLOUR VARIETIES

King Charles—Black and tan.
Ruby—Red.
Prince Charles—Tricolour.
Blenheim—Chestnut and white.

In 1932, the four varieties were classified as King Charles Spaniels and have remained such. Will Judy, in the *Dog Encyclopaedia*, noted that 'Where there are colour classifications, the quality suffers because breeders seek colour rather than quality.' Freeman Lloyd opines, 'Fashions in toy dogs change almost as often as styles in dress!'

Queen Victoria's favourite King Charles Spaniel, Dash, was painted by Landseer.

was said that the Duke acquired his first pair of spaniels from China. The Blenheim spaniels were bred by the Marlborough Dukes for years, and they were considered to be the best and the smallest of the toy spaniels.

The toy spaniel always has been a popular toy dog in England. By 1861, classes for toy dogs were held at the Birmingham dog show, two years after the first classes were held for gundogs. In 1885, the Toy Spaniel Club was formed, and the dogs were divided by colour and a standard for the breed was drafted. It called for a compact and cobby body with a wide and deep chest, a well-domed head, a massive skull, a short nose and a deep stop. It was to have a long, straight and silky coat with heavy feathering on the legs, ears and tail. The standard has changed very little over the years, except to clarify certain points. In 1923, the colours were reclassified under one breed name and, since that time, all colours have competed together for the Best of Breed award.

Queen Victoria also was an ardent admirer of the breed and owned a spaniel called Dash. Another dog, Darmail Wild, won over 100 firsts at shows during Victorian times.

The Cavalier King Charles Spaniel is a separate breed with a very similar history. The Cavalier originally was classified with the toy spaniels. In 1928, it became a breed of its own and its name changed to the Cavalier. The Cavalier is a larger and heavier dog than the King Charles Spaniel, longer in foreface and with a jaw more like the Cocker Spaniel than the Pekingese.

The toy spaniels were well known in the US, starting in the

A LASTING IMPRINT: THE THUMB MARK

The Blenheim (white and chestnut) has the much desired 'thumb mark' on its forehead. Legend has it that while the Duke was in battle, his wife Sarah sat with a spaniel bitch, who was in whelp, on her lap. In her nervousness, the Duchess pressed her thumb on the bitch's head and when the puppies were whelped, all had a chestnut-coloured spot on their foreheads the size of a thumb.

THE OTHER TOY SPANIEL
When distinguishing between the King Charles Spaniel and the Cavalier King Charles Spaniel, remember that the King Charles Spaniel has the shorter muzzle thus the shorter name! But also remember that the Cavalier is a larger dog [5.4–8.2 kgs (12–18 lbs)], than the King Charles, whose weight runs between 3.6–6.3 kgs (8–14 lbs). Both dogs have the same colour combinations, but the King Charles has the pug-type muzzle.

early 1800s. In fact, it was noted on the billing for the Mayflower's voyage to America that there was a 'Spannell' on board.

The English Toy Spaniel, as the breed is known in the US, was first registered there in 1902, and all varieties and colours came under the designation of this new name. In the early 1900s, Mrs Senn of New York City owned three well-known dogs, Ch Perseverance, Ch Square Face and Ch Romeo. Mrs Raymond Mallock imported the famous English dog Ch Rollo, and he quickly gained his American Kennel Club championship. By the mid-20th century, Viggo Nielsen

of Brooklyn, New York; Oral Landon of Michigan; Mrs George Homburg of St. Paul, Minnesota and Mrs Julia Whelan of New York all had well-known kennels. At the present time, the breed in US falls in the bottom 25% of American Kennel Club (AKC) breeds in popularity.

In 1930, Will Judy wrote, 'Perhaps the epitaph of the breed was first written when the fad for short noses pushed-up between the eyes became the "go" of the breeders. Then, the breed lost its resemblance to the general spaniel family. Here is the case of a worthy small dog that finds its worst enemy in its supposed friends, its breeder.' Mr Judy's prediction certainly has proven worthless. In the 21st century, the King Charles Spaniel remains a beloved pure-bred dog with a steady following around the world.

Displaying red and white coloration are a King Charles Spaniel and a Cavalier King Charles Spaniel.

From the US, an example of the Blenheim variety of the English Toy Spaniel, as the breed is called in that country.

Characteristics of the
KING CHARLES SPANIEL

The King Charles Spaniel is a wonderful little dog! He is not only aristocratic but also cute and smart. Several of them can easily live with you in a small flat as well as ride next to you in the car. They are easy to carry on trains or tubes, as they will fit in small baskets or carriers. Your King Charles can travel on an aeroplane in a small crate that will fit under your seat. In addition, they eat little compared to larger breeds and clean-up chores are also considerably easier! The King Charles is a quick learner and, in a short period of time, your little pup will turn into a charming gentleman or lady that will be a joy to live with.

Unlike the gundogs from which the King Charles derives, he is small and will not be a companion for a two-km run or a ten-lap swim around the pool. He will not chase down rabbits and he will not pick up fallen birds. However, if you like a small, sophisticated dog who is easy to live with, easy to maintain and who will be your companion for life, then you are looking in the right place. Once you give your heart and home to a King Charles Spaniel, you will remain a devotee of the breed for a lifetime.

If you have young children in your household at the time that you purchase your puppy, you must be certain that they are aware that this is a small dog and that he will remain so for his lifetime. This is not a dog suited to rough-and-tumble play as would be a sporting dog like a Golden Retriever or a Springer Spaniel. The King Charles weighs no more than 6.3 kgs (14 lbs) as an adult and he should be handled with care. He must not be dropped, sat upon or pushed around.

The King Charles has a steady disposition and fits in easily with

The King Charles' small size enables him to fit into any home. Add to that the breed's delightful personality and distinguished looks, and you may find it hard to stop at just one!

family life. He gets on well with children and will accept strangers once he has had a chance to look them over. He can also be a good little indoor watchdog. The breed is clean and quiet, and has a soft and appealing expression. They are elegant, cheerful, very affectionate and devoted companions. They are sweet and delicate due to size, but they are also sturdy. They have a selfless temperament and an ego-less disposition. What more could you want in a little companion?

THE DECISION TO BUY A PURE-BRED DOG

Certainly the appearance and character of the distinctive King Charles Spaniel have captured your fancy, and thus you are considering the purchase of a pure-bred dog. There are many predictable traits that recommend pure-bred dogs over mixed-breed dogs. It is almost impossible to determine what a mixed-breed puppy will look like as an adult. More importantly, it is impossible to determine what the temperament of a puppy of mixed parentage is going to be like. Will he be suitable for the person or family who wishes to own him? If the puppy grows up to be too big, too hairy or too active for the owner, what then will happen?

Size and temperament can vary to a degree, even within pure-bred dogs. Still, controlled breeding over many generations has produced dogs that give us reasonable assurance of what a pure-bred puppy will look and act like when he reaches maturity. This predictability is more important than you might think.

Just about any dog whose background is made up of sound individuals has the potential to be a loving companion. However, the predictability of a pure-bred dog offers reasonable insurance that the dog will suit not only the person's aesthetic demands but also the owner's lifestyle. Before you bring a King Charles Spaniel puppy into your household, visit breeders and spend as much time with both puppies and adults as

DO YOU WANT TO LIVE LONGER?
If you like to volunteer, it is wonderful if you can take your dog to a nursing home once a week for several hours. The elder community loves to have a dog with which to visit, and often your dog will bring a bit of companionship to someone who is lonely or somewhat detached from the world. You will be not only bringing happiness to someone else but also keeping your dog busy—and we haven't even mentioned the fact that it has been discovered that volunteering helps to increase your own longevity!

If you're always on the go, your King Charles Spaniel can join you! Easy portability is yet another plus with this compact toy dog.

you can. You must confirm that the adult King Charles Spaniel is the dog that appeals to you aesthetically and temperamentally, and above all, be certain that you will in fact be a suitable owner for the breed.

HEALTH CONSIDERATIONS FOR THE KING CHARLES SPANIEL

All pure-bred dogs are predisposed to some hereditary health concerns, and the King Charles is no exception. As a prospective owner of this breed, you should be aware of these potential problems and understand what they are about. By buying your puppy from a reputable breeder who is knowledgeable about these problems, you are making the most responsible first step possible. Openly discuss all of the following with your chosen breeder.

LUXATED KNEECAPS OR PATELLAR LUXATION

Common to most small breeds, this is an important problem and it has been reported for well over 100 years in the King Charles. However, due to careful breeding, as this is usually an inherited fault, the fault is not as prominent as it was at one time. The patella, or kneecap, deviates to the inside of the leg so that the muscles of the leg responsible for straightening the knee are no longer in alignment. This can result in little or no lameness or complete non-use of the leg.

Conditions that cause this condition are a shallow groove, weak ligaments and/or misalignment of the tendons and muscles that straighten the knee joint. The patella can then slip either inward or outward. Your veterinary surgeon should be contacted if you suspect that your dog has this problem. The vet will manipulate the stifle joint to see if he can push the kneecap in or out of position. Your vet should determine if your dog is a candidate for surgery.

UMBILICAL HERNIA OR INGUINAL HERNIA

An hernia is a protrusion of an organ or part of an organ through an opening in the abdominal wall that would normally close with growth. This is a fairly common fault and can be seen at birth or by two weeks of age. This is a common surgery and can take place at an early age for repair.

INCOMPLETE FONTANEL CLOSURE

This is a soft spot on the skull that remains open even after maturity. All puppies are born with this soft spot, which usually closes as the dog grows. With a dog with a head as large as that of the King Charles, this is a significant concern for breeders. Again, your vet should be contacted about this problem.

CORRECTIVE SURGERY

Surgery is often used to correct genetic bone diseases in dogs. Usually the problems present themselves early in the dog's life and must be treated before bone growth stops.

DIABETES MELLITUS

This can affect middle-aged to older bitches. Early signs of diabetes are frequent urination, drinking lots of water, a large appetite or an unexplained weight loss. With early diagnosis and proper care, life for the dog can be prolonged.

BREATHING DIFFICULTIES

The King Charles Spaniel has a pushed-in nose like the Pekingese or Japanese Chin. These breeds have abnormally small openings to the nostrils and relatively long palates. Dogs prefer to breathe through their noses and, for these breeds, it becomes difficult to breathe through the small nasal openings. Thus, the dog must increase his respiratory effort even when at rest.

Because of their breathing problems, King Charles Spaniels can be very susceptible to heat and cold; caution must be taken, particularly in the summer months. Your dog must never be given strenuous activity in the heat and he must not be out in the cold any longer than necessary.

Abnormal noises, such as snorting and snoring, are also common with these breeds.

Although this list of health problems may look daunting, King Charles Spaniels are still considered to be an healthy breed. The problems mentioned are possible in the breed and a buyer should be aware of them. Some of these diseases are rare and most of them only turn up on occasion. Do not be turned away from the breed but do be aware that if the breeder of your puppy is reputable, and thus aware of these problems, he will be doing his best to breed them out of his line, never using a carrier of an hereditary disease as a breeding animal.

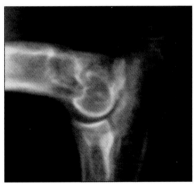

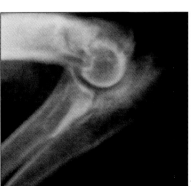

X-rays showing dogs' knee joints, including their kneecaps (patellas). Patellar luxation has been an inherited problem in the breed for more than a century, but careful breeding continues to lessen its incidence.

Breed Standard for the
KING CHARLES SPANIEL

The breed standard is a written description of what is believed to be the perfect specimen of a breed. A standard is required for every pure-bred breed of dog. The standard gives breeders and judges a mental image of what the ideal representative of the breed should look like. Reputable breeders, therefore, strive to produce animals that will meet the qualifications depicted in the standard. Judges use the standard to determine whether the dogs presented in the show ring conform to the standard. The dog that most closely conforms to the standard, in the judge's opinion, is the Best of Breed for the day. This is the concept that governs conformation shows.

A well-bred King Charles Spaniel should look like a proper spaniel and he will have the personality, disposition and intelligence that are sought after in the breed. The standard details the breed's physical attributes (head, mouth, neck, colour, coat, etc.) as well as the breed's temperament, characteristics and movement or gait.

Standards originally were written by fanciers who had a love and a concern for the breed. These early dog fanciers, many of whom were horse people who knew mammal anatomy and took much of the terminology for

granted, understood the basics of proper construction. These people also recognised that the essential characteristics of the King Charles Spaniel were unlike those of any other breed and that care (through a written breeding and judging standard) must be taken that these characteristics were maintained through the generations.

As time progressed, new generations of dog folk needed more details to better understand canine construction. Most of the new blood were not horse people. Thus, breeders became more aware that certain areas of the dog needed a better description, and they would meet together and work out a revised, more detailed, standard. Standards change very little over the years and are never revised a whim. Serious study and exchange between experts and breeders take place before any move is made. In Britain, The Kennel Club has the final word on alterations to any of the standards that it safeguards. In the US, the recognised national parent club controls the standard for the breed.

The American Kennel Club standard is quite similar to the British standard, though it is much more detailed. It is worth a look-see. The 'General Appearance,' as set forth in the AKC standard, reads thusly: 'The English Toy Spaniel is a compact, cobby and essentially square dog possessed of a short nose, domed head, a merry and affectionate demeanor and a silky, flowing coat. His compact, sturdy body and charming temperament, together with his rounded head, lustrous dark eye, and well cushioned face, proclaim him a dog of distinction and character.'

The important characteristics of the breed are exemplified by the head. The AKC standard describes the head as follows:

A young Ruby with a beautiful head that exemplifies the points in the standard: 'skull large,' 'well-domed,' and 'full over eyes.' Also displayed are the characteristic upturned nose and large, wide-set, dark eyes.

A study in colour, with each variety represented: Ruby, Prince Charles, King Charles and Blenheim.

'Head large in comparison to size, with a plush, chubby look, albeit with a degree of refinement which prevents it from being coarse.' The skull is 'high and well domed; from the side, curves as far out over the eyes as possible.' The stop is 'deep and well defined.' The muzzle is 'very short, with the nose well laid back and with well developed cushioning under the eyes.' The jaw is 'square, broad, and deep, and well turned up, with lips properly meeting to give a finished appearance.' The bite is 'slightly undershot; teeth not to show. A wry mouth should be penalized; a hanging tongue is extremely objectionable.'

THE KENNEL CLUB STANDARD FOR THE KING CHARLES SPANIEL

General Appearance: Refined, compact and cobby.

Characteristics: Happy, intelligent toy spaniel, with distinctive domed head.

Temperament: Reserved, gentle and affectionate.

Head and Skull: Skull large in comparison to size, well domed, full over eyes. Nose black with large, wide-open nostrils, very short and turned up to meet skull. Stop between skull and nose well defined. Muzzle square, wide and deep, well turned up, lower jaw wide, lips exactly meeting, giving nice finish. Cheeks not falling away under eyes, but well cushioned.

Eyes: Very large and dark, set wide apart, eyelids block square to face line, pleasing expression.

Ears: Set-on low, hanging quite flat to cheeks, very long and well feathered.

Mouth: Bite should be slightly undershot. Protruding tongue highly undesirable.

Neck: Of medium length; arched giving proud carriage of head.

Forequarters: Legs short, straight. Shoulders well laid back, elbows close to rib cage, turning neither in nor out.

Body: Chest wide and deep, back short and level.

Hindquarters: Sufficient muscle to give positive driving movement, stifles well bent, hocks well let down and defined. Straight when viewed from behind, turning neither in nor out.

Feet: Compact, well padded and feathered, toes well knuckled, round cat-shaped foot, well cushioned, pasterns firm. Occasionally central pads and nails fused together.

Tail: Well feathered, not carried over or above level of back. Docking optional.

Gait/Movement: Free, active and elegant, driving from behind. Sound movement highly desirable.

Coat: Long, silky and straight, slight wave allowed, never curly.

Legs, ears and tail profusely feathered.

Colour: *Black and Tan:* rich glossy black, with bright mahogany-tan markings on muzzle, legs, chest, linings of ears, under tail and spots over eyes. White patch on chest undesirable.

Tricolour: ground pearly white, with well distributed black patches, brilliant tan markings on cheeks, linings of ears, under tail and spots over eyes. Wide white blaze between eyes and up forehead.

Blenheim: ground pearly white, with well distributed chestnut-red patches. Wide, clear blaze with the 'spot' in centre of skull, should be a clear chestnut-red mark about the size of a penny.

Ruby: whole coloured, rich chestnut red. White patch on chest highly undesirable.

Size: Weight: 3.6–6.3 kgs (8–14 lbs).

Faults: Any departure from the foregoing points should be considered a fault and the seriousness with which the fault should be regarded should be in exact proportion to its degree.

Note: Male animals should have two apparently normal testicles fully descended into the scrotum.

A puppy inherits many traits, both in looks and in temperament, from its parents. Observing at least one of the parents is an aid in predicting how your puppy will mature.

KING CHARLES SPANIEL

WHERE TO BEGIN?

If you are convinced that the King Charles Spaniel is the ideal dog for you, it's time to learn about where to find a puppy and what to look for. Locating a litter of King Charles Spaniels should not present a problem for the new owner. You should enquire about breeders in your area who enjoy a good reputation in the breed. Although the breed is not numerically strong in most countries, it is possible to locate dedicated breeders with a minimum of effort. Fortunately, the majority of King Charles Spaniel breeders are devoted to the breed and its well-being. The Kennel Club is able to recommend breeders of quality King Charles Spaniels, as can any local all-breed club or King Charles Spaniel club. New owners should have little problem finding a reputable breeder who doesn't live on the other side of the country (or in a different country).

Potential owners are encouraged to attend dog shows to see the King Charles Spaniels in person, to meet the owners and handlers firsthand and to get an

PUPPY APPEARANCE

Your puppy should have a well-fed appearance but not a distended abdomen, which may indicate worms or incorrect feeding, or both. The body should be firm, with a solid feel. The skin of the abdomen should be pale pink and clean, without signs of scratching or rash. Check the hind legs to make certain that dewclaws were removed, if any were present at birth.

idea of what King Charles Spaniels look like outside a photographer's lens. Provided you approach the handlers when they are not terribly busy with the

PUPPY SELECTION

Your selection of a good puppy can be determined by your needs. A show potential or a good pet? It is your choice. Every puppy, however, should be of good temperament. Although show-quality puppies are bred and raised with emphasis on physical conformation, responsible breeders strive for equally good temperament. Do not buy from a breeder who concentrates solely on physical beauty at the expense of personality.

INSURANCE

Many good breeders will offer you insurance with your new puppy, which is an excellent idea. The first few weeks of insurance will probably be covered free of charge or with only minimal cost, allowing you to take up the policy when this expires. If you own a dog, it is sensible to take out such a policy as veterinary fees can be high, although routine vaccinations and boosters are not covered. Look carefully at the many options available to you before deciding which suits you best.

dogs, most are more than willing to answer questions, recommend breeders and give advice.

Once you have contacted and met a breeder or two and made your choice about which breeder is best suited to your needs, it's time to visit the litter. Since you are likely to be choosing a King Charles Spaniel as a pet dog and not a show dog, you simply should select a pup that is friendly, attractive and healthy. King Charles Spaniels generally have small litters, averaging four puppies, so selection is limited once you have located a desirable litter.

Unlike most breeds of dog, the King Charles has an undershot bite, and this will be evident in a young puppy. The colour of the puppy is another consideration, as there are four attractive varieties in the breed: solid red, black and tan, tricoloured and chestnut and white. Each variety has its own appeal. Discuss colours with the breeder. Some varieties may be easier to acquire in certain regions, while others may require a bit more patience until an available puppy arrives. There is

DOCUMENTATION

Two important documents you will get from the breeder are the pup's pedigree and registration certificate. The breeder should register the litter and each pup with The Kennel Club, and it is necessary for you to have the paperwork if you plan on showing or breeding in the future.

Make sure you know the breeder's intentions on which type of registration he will obtain for the pup. There are limited registrations that may prohibit the dog from being shown, bred or competing in non-conformation trials such as Obedience or Agility if the breeder feels that the pup is not of sufficient quality to do so. There is also a type of registration that will permit the dog in non-conformation competition only.

On the reverse side of the registration certificate, the new owner can find the transfer section, which must be signed by the breeder.

YOUR SCHEDULE . . .

If you lead an erratic, unpredictable life, with daily or weekly changes in your work requirements, consider the problems of owning a dog. The new puppy has to be fed regularly, socialised (loved, petted, handled, introduced to other people) and, most importantly, allowed to visit outdoors for toilet training. As the dog gets older, it can be more tolerant of deviations in its feeding and toilet relief.

no difference in character or health between the varieties.

Breeders commonly allow visitors to see their litters by

A look at the pups' quarters tells volumes about the care they are receiving from the breeder. Good care also is evident in clear eyes, shiny coats, alert temperaments and the overall impression of health.

around the fifth or sixth week, and puppies leave for their new homes around the ninth or tenth week. King Charles puppies are especially fragile and should not be released any earlier. Breeders who permit their puppies to leave early are more interested in your pounds than in their puppies' well-being. Puppies need to learn the rules of the pack from their dams, and most dams continue teaching the pups manners and dos and don'ts until around the eighth week. Breeders spend significant amounts of time with the King Charles Spaniel toddlers so that the pups are able to interact with the 'other species,' i.e. humans. Given the long history that dogs and humans have, bonding between the two species is natural but must be nurtured. A well-bred, well-socialised King Charles Spaniel pup wants nothing more than to be near you and please you.

COMMITMENT OF OWNERSHIP

After considering all of these factors, you have most likely already made some very important decisions about selecting your puppy. You have chosen a King Charles Spaniel, which means that you have decided which characteristics you want in a dog and what type of dog will best fit into your family and lifestyle. If you have selected a breeder, you have gone a step further—you have done your research and found a responsible, conscientious person who breeds quality King Charles Spaniels and who should be a reliable source of help as you and your puppy adjust to life together. If you have observed a litter in action, you have obtained a firsthand look at the dynamics of a puppy 'pack' and, thus, you have learned about each pup's individual personality—perhaps you have even found one that particularly appeals to you.

BOY OR GIRL?

An important consideration to be discussed is the sex of your puppy. For a family companion, a bitch may be the better choice, considering the female's inbred concern for all young creatures and her accompanying tolerance and patience. It is always advisable to spay a pet bitch or neuter a pet male, which may guarantee your King Charles Spaniel a longer life.

However, even if you have not yet found the King Charles Spaniel puppy of your dreams, observing pups will help you learn to recognise certain behaviour and to determine what a pup's behaviour indicates about his temperament. You will be able to pick out which pups are the leaders, which ones are less outgoing, which ones are confident, which ones are shy, playful, friendly, aggressive, etc. Equally as important, you will learn to recognise what an healthy pup should look and act like. All of these things will help you in your search, and when you find the King Charles Spaniel that was meant for you, you will know it!

Researching your breed, selecting a responsible breeder and observing as many pups as possible are all important steps on the way to dog ownership. It may

seem like a lot of effort…and you have not even taken the pup home yet! Remember, though, you cannot be too careful when it comes to deciding on the type of dog you want and finding out about your prospective pup's background. Buying a puppy is not—or should not be—just another whimsical purchase. This is one instance in which you actually do get to choose your own family!

You may be thinking that buying a puppy should be fun—it should not be so serious and so much work. Keep in mind that your puppy is not a cuddly stuffed toy or decorative lawn ornament; rather, he is a living creature that will become a real member of your family. You will come to realise that, while buying a puppy is a pleasurable and exciting endeavour, it is not something to be taken lightly.

Not all colours are available from every breeder, but, with such a selection, how will you choose?

All pups should be alert and friendly, but some may need a bit more coaxing to come out and play.

Relax...the fun will start when the pup comes home!

Always keep in mind that a puppy is nothing more than a baby in a furry disguise...a baby who is virtually helpless in a human world and who trusts his owner for fulfilment of his basic needs for survival. In addition to food, water and shelter, your pup needs care, protection, guidance and love. If you are not prepared to commit to this, then you are not prepared to own a dog.

'Wait a minute,' you say. 'How hard could this be? All of my neighbours own dogs and they seem to be doing just fine. Why should I have to worry about all of this?' Well, you should not worry about it; in fact, you will probably find that once your King Charles Spaniel pup gets used to his new home, he will fall into his place in the family quite naturally. However, it never hurts to emphasise the commitment of dog ownership. With some time and patience, it is really not too difficult to raise a curious and happy King Charles Spaniel pup to be a well-adjusted and well-mannered adult dog—a dog that could be your most loyal friend.

PREPARING PUPPY'S PLACE IN YOUR HOME

Researching your breed and finding a breeder are only two aspects of the 'homework' you will have to do before taking your King Charles Spaniel puppy home. You will also have to prepare your home and family for the new addition. Much as you would prepare a nursery for a newborn baby, you will need to designate a place in your home that will be the puppy's own. How you prepare your home will depend on how much freedom the dog will be allowed. Whatever you decide, you must ensure that he has a place that he can 'call his own.'

DID YOU KNOW?
You should not even think about buying a puppy that looks sick, undernourished, overly frightened or nervous. Sometimes a timid puppy will warm up to you after a 30-minute 'let's-get-acquainted' session.

When you take your new puppy into your home, you are bringing him into what will become his home as well. Obviously, you did not buy a puppy with the intentions of catering to his every whim and allowing him to 'rule the roost,' but, in order for a puppy to grow into a stable, well-adjusted dog, he has to feel comfortable in his surroundings. Remember, he is leaving the warmth and security of his mother and littermates, as well as the familiarity of the only place he has ever known, so it is important to make his transition as easy as possible. By preparing a place in your home for the puppy, you are making him feel as welcome as possible in a strange new place. It should not take him long to get used to it, but the sudden shock of being transplanted is somewhat traumatic for a young pup. Imagine how a small child would feel in the same situation— that is how your puppy must be feeling. It is up to you to reassure him and to let him know, 'Little chap, you are going to like it here!'

WHAT YOU SHOULD BUY

CRATE

To someone unfamiliar with the use of crates in dog training, it may seem like punishment to shut a dog in a crate, but this is not the case at all. Although all breeders do not advocate crate training, more and more breeders and trainers are recommending crates as preferred tools for show puppies as well as pet puppies.

Crates are not cruel—crates have many humane and highly effective uses in dog care and training. For example, crate training is a very popular and very successful house-training method. In addition, a crate can keep your dog safe during travel and, perhaps most importantly, a crate provides your dog with a place of his own in your home. It serves as a 'doggie bedroom' of

ARE YOU A FIT OWNER?
If the breeder from whom you are buying a puppy asks you a lot of personal questions, do not be insulted. Such a breeder wants to be sure that you will be a fit provider for his puppy.

Your local pet shop will carry a variety of suitable crates; a small sized crate will accommodate your King Charles throughout his life.

PHOTO COURTESY OF DOSKOCIL

than what his early ancestors enjoyed.

As far as purchasing a crate, the type that you buy is up to you. It will most likely be one of the two most popular types: wire or fibreglass. There are advantages and disadvantages to each type. For example, a wire crate is more open, allowing the air to flow through and affording the dog a view of what is going on around

sorts—your King Charles Spaniel can curl up in his crate when he wants to sleep or when he just needs a break. Many dogs sleep in their crates overnight. With soft bedding and his favourite toy, a crate becomes a cosy pseudo-den for your dog. Like his ancestors, he too will seek out the comfort and retreat of a den—you just happen to be providing him with something a little more luxurious

PREPARING FOR PUP

Unfortunately, when a puppy is bought by someone who does not take into consideration the time and attention that dog ownership requires, it is the puppy who suffers when he is either abandoned or placed in a shelter by a frustrated owner. So all of the 'homework' you do in preparation for your pup's arrival will benefit you both. The more informed you are, the more you will know what to expect and the better equipped you will be to handle the ups and downs of raising a puppy. Hopefully, everyone in the household is willing to do his part in raising and caring for the pup. The anticipation of owning a dog often brings a lot of promises from excited family members: 'I will walk him every day,' 'I will feed him,' 'I will house-train him,' etc., but these things take time and effort, and promises can be easily forgotten once the novelty of the new pet has worn off.

CRATE TRAINING TIPS

During crate training, you should partition off the section of the crate in which the pup stays. If he is given too big an area, this will hinder your training efforts. Crate training is based on the fact that a dog does not like to soil his sleeping quarters, so it is ineffective to keep a pup in a crate that is so big that he can eliminate in one end and get far enough away from it to sleep. Also, you want to make the crate den-like for the pup. Blankets and a favourite toy will make the crate cosy for the small pup; as he grows, you may want to evict some of his 'roommates' to make more room. It will take some coaxing at first, but be patient. Given some time to get used to it, your pup will adapt to his new home-within-an-home quite nicely.

twigs, etc. that the pup would use in the wild to make a den; the pup can make his own 'burrow' in the crate. Although your pup is far removed from his den-making ancestors, the denning instinct is still a part of his genetic makeup. Second, until you take your pup home, he has been sleeping amid the warmth of his mother and littermates. While a blanket is not the same as a warm, breathing body, it still provides heat and something with which to snuggle. You will want to wash your pup's bedding frequently in case he has a toileting accident in his crate, and replace or remove any blanket that becomes ragged and starts to fall apart.

him, while a fibreglass crate is sturdier. Both can double as travel crates, providing protection for the dog. Purchase a small crate for your King Charles, which should give him room to stand up and lie down comfortably, and will suit him both as a puppy and when fully-grown.

BEDDING

Veterinary bedding in the dog's crate will help the dog feel more at home, and you may also like to pop in a small blanket. First, this will take the place of the leaves,

Some crates easily can fit a small pack of King Charles, but crate training only works if each dog has his own personal crate, a 'den' of his own.

TOYS, TOYS, TOYS!

With a big variety of dog toys available, and so many that look like they would be a lot of fun for a dog, be careful in your selection. It is amazing what a set of puppy teeth can do to an innocent-looking toy, so, obviously, safety is a major consideration. Be sure to choose the most durable products that you can find. Hard nylon bones and toys are a safe bet, and many of them are offered in different scents and flavours that will be sure to capture your dog's attention. It is always fun to play a game of catch with your dog, and there are balls and flying discs that are specially made to withstand dog teeth.

Toys

Toys are a must for dogs of all ages, especially for curious playful pups. Puppies are the 'children' of the dog world, and what child does not love toys? Chew toys provide enjoyment for both dog and owner—your dog will enjoy playing with his favourite toys, while you will enjoy the fact that they distract him from chewing on your expensive shoes and leather sofa. Puppies love to chew; in fact, chewing is a physical need for pups as they are teething, and everything looks appetising! The full range of your possessions— from old tea towel to Oriental carpet—are fair game in the eyes of a teething pup. Puppies are not all that discerning when it comes to finding something literally to 'sink their teeth into'—everything tastes great!

King Charles Spaniel puppies like soft toys. King Charles generally are not very energetic chewers and should not be too problematic in this regard. Squeaky toys are quite popular and should only be offered under careful supervision. If a pup 'disembowels' one of these, the small plastic squeaker inside can be dangerous if swallowed. Monitor the condition of all your pup's toys carefully and get rid of any that have been chewed to the point of becoming potentially dangerous.

Be careful of natural bones, which have a tendency to splinter into sharp, dangerous pieces. Also be careful of rawhide, which can turn into pieces that are easy to swallow and become a mushy mess on your carpet.

LEAD

A nylon lead is probably the best option, as it is the most resistant to puppy teeth should your pup take a liking to chewing on his lead. Of course, this is an habit that should be nipped in the bud, but, if your pup likes to chew on his lead, he has a very slim chance of being able to chew through the strong nylon. Nylon leads are also lightweight, which

CHEWING TIPS

Chewing goes hand in hand with nipping in the sense that a teething puppy is always looking for a way to soothe his aching gums. In this case, instead of chewing on you, he may have taken a liking to your favourite shoe or something else that he should not be chewing. Again, realise that this is a normal canine behaviour that does not need to be discouraged, only redirected. Your pup just needs to be taught what is acceptable to chew on and what is off-limits. Consistently tell him NO when you catch him chewing on something forbidden and give him a chew toy.

Conversely, praise him when you catch him chewing on something appropriate. In this way, you are discouraging the inappropriate behaviour and reinforcing the desired behaviour. The puppy chewing should stop after his adult teeth have come in, but an adult dog continues to chew for various reasons—perhaps because he is bored, needs to relieve tension or just likes to chew. That is why it is important to redirect his chewing when he is still young.

Don't forget the toys! Soft toys seem to be the chew of choice for the King Charles, both in puppyhood and adulthood.

Pet shops usually stock a wide assortment of leads. A lightweight yet sturdy nylon lead will suit your King Charles' needs.

is good for a young King Charles Spaniel who is just getting used to the idea of walking on a lead.

For everyday walking and safety purposes, the nylon lead is a good choice. As your pup grows up and gets used to walking on the lead, you may want to purchase a flexible lead, which allows you to extend the length to give the dog a broader area to explore or to shorten the length to keep the dog near you.

COLLAR
Your pup should get used to wearing a collar all the time

since you will want to attach his ID tags to it; plus, you have to attach the lead to something! A lightweight nylon collar is a good choice. Make certain that the collar fits snugly enough so that the pup cannot wriggle out of it, but is loose enough so that it will not be uncomfortably tight around the pup's neck. You should be able to fit a finger between the pup's neck and the collar. It may take some time for your pup to get used to wearing the collar, but soon he will not even notice that it is there.

FOOD AND WATER BOWLS

Your pup will need two bowls, one for food and one for water. You may want two sets of bowls, one for indoors and one for outdoors, depending on where the dog will be fed and where he will be spending time. Stainless steel or sturdy plastic bowls are popular choices. Plastic bowls are more chewable, though this is not a problem with the King Charles. The steel variety is preferred by many owners because the bowls can be sterilised. It is important to buy sturdy bowls that will last the lifetime of your dog.

CLEANING SUPPLIES

Until a pup is house-trained, you will be doing a lot of cleaning. 'Accidents' will occur, which is acceptable in the beginning stages

Purchase durable, easily cleaned food and water bowls, in small sizes, for your King Charles Spaniel.

PHOTO COURTESY OF MIKKI PET PRODUCTS.

CHOOSE AN APPROPRIATE COLLAR

The **BUCKLE COLLAR** is the standard collar used for everyday purposes. Be sure that you adjust the buckle on growing puppies. Check it every day. It can become too tight overnight! These collars can be made of leather or nylon. Attach your dog's identification tags to this collar.

The **CHOKE COLLAR** is constructed of highly polished steel so that it slides easily through the stainless steel loop. The idea is that the dog controls the pressure around its neck and he will stop pulling if the collar becomes uncomfortable. It is *not* suitable for use on Toy dogs.

The **HARNESS or HALTER** is for a trained dog that has to be restrained to prevent running away, chasing a cat and the like. Considered the most humane of all restraining devices, it is frequently used on smaller dogs for which collars are not comfortable.

of toilet training because the puppy does not know any better. All you can do is be prepared to clean up any accidents as soon as they happen. Old rags, towels, newspapers and a safe disinfectant are good to have on hand.

BEYOND THE BASICS
The items previously discussed are the bare necessities. You will find out what else you need as you go along—grooming supplies, flea/tick protection, baby gates to partition a room, etc. These things will vary depending on your situation, but it is important that you have everything you need to feed and make your King Charles Spaniel comfortable in his first few days at home.

PUPPY-PROOFING YOUR HOME
Aside from making sure that your King Charles Spaniel will be comfortable in your home, you also have to make sure that your home is safe for your King Charles Spaniel. This means taking

TEETHING TIP
Puppies like soft toys for chewing. Because they are teething, soft items like stuffed toys soothe their aching gums, but be sure to monitor your pup when he's playing with a potentially destructible (and thus potentially dangerous) toy.

precautions that your pup will not get into anything he should not get into and that there is nothing within his reach that may harm him should he sniff it, chew it, inspect it, etc. This probably seems obvious since, while you are primarily concerned with your pup's safety, at the same time you do not want your belongings to be ruined. Breakables should be placed out of reach if your dog is to have full run of the house. If he is to be limited to certain places within the house, keep any potentially dangerous items in the 'off-limits' areas.

CHEMICAL TOXINS
Scour your garage for potential puppy dangers. Remove weed killers, pesticides and antifreeze materials. Antifreeze is highly toxic and even a few drops can kill a puppy or adult dog. The sweet taste attracts the animal, who will quickly consume it from the floor or kerbside.

An electrical lead can pose a danger should the puppy decide to taste it—and who is going to convince a pup that it would not make a great chew toy? Leads should be fastened tightly against the wall. If your dog is going to spend time in a crate, make sure that there is nothing near his crate that he can reach if he sticks his

PUPPY-PROOFING
Thoroughly puppy-proof your house before bringing your puppy home. Never use cockroach or rodent poisons in any area that will be accessible to the dog. Avoid the use of toilet cleaners. Most dogs are born with 'toilet sonar' and will take a drink if the lid is left open. Also keep the rubbish secured and out of reach.

NATURAL TOXINS
Examine your grass and garden landscaping before bringing your puppy home. Many varieties of plants have leaves, stems or flowers that are toxic if ingested, and you can depend on a curious puppy to investigate them. Ask your vet for information on poisonous plants or research them at your library.

curious little nose or paws through the openings. Just as you would with a child, keep all household cleaners and chemicals where the pup cannot reach them.

It is also important to make sure that the outside of your home is safe. Of course, your puppy should never be unsupervised, but a pup let loose in the garden will want to run and explore, and he should be granted that freedom in your fenced garden. Be certain that your fence is secure and always repair any gaps that you notice in the fence. Fortunately, King Charles Spaniels are not much interested in digging and should not try to 'escape' in this manner.

FIRST TRIP TO THE VET
You have selected your puppy, and your home and family are ready. Now all you have to do is collect your King Charles Spaniel from the breeder and the fun begins, right? Well...not so fast.

Something else you need to plan is your pup's first trip to the veterinary surgeon. Perhaps the breeder can recommend someone in the area who specialises in toy dogs, or maybe you know some other King Charles Spaniel owners who can suggest a good vet. Either way, you should have an appointment arranged for your pup before you pick him up.

The pup's first visit will consist of an overall examination to make sure that the pup does not have any problems that are not apparent to you. The veterinary surgeon will also set up a schedule for the pup's vaccinations; the breeder will inform you of which ones the pup has already received and the vet can continue from there.

INTRODUCTION TO THE FAMILY

Everyone in the house will be excited about the puppy's coming home and will want to pet him and play with him, but it is best to make the introduction low-key so as not to overwhelm the puppy. He is apprehensive already. It is the first time he has been separated from his mother and the breeder, and the ride to your home is likely to be the first time he has been in a car. The last thing you want to do is smother him, as this will only frighten him further. This is not to say that human contact is not

TOXIC PLANTS
Many plants can be toxic to dogs. If you see your dog carrying a piece of vegetation in his mouth, approach him in a quiet, disinterested manner, avoid eye contact, pet him and gradually remove the plant from his mouth. Alternatively, offer him a treat and maybe he'll drop the plant on his own accord. Be sure no toxic plants are growing in your own garden.

extremely necessary at this stage, because this is the time when a connection between the pup and his human family is formed. Gentle petting and soothing words should help console him, as well as just putting him down and letting him explore on his own (under your watchful eye, of course).

The pup may approach the family members or may busy himself with exploring for a

FEEDING TIPS

You will probably start feeding your pup the same food that he has been getting from the breeder; the breeder should give you a few days' supply to start you off. Although you should not give your pup too many treats, you will want to have puppy treats on hand for coaxing, training, rewards, etc. Be careful, though, as a small pup's calorie requirements are relatively low and a few treats can add up to almost a full day's worth of calories without the required nutrition.

while. Gradually, each person should spend some time with the pup, one at a time, crouching down to get as close to the pup's level as possible, letting him sniff their hands and petting him gently. He definitely needs human attention and he needs to be touched—this is how to form an immediate bond. Just remember that the pup is experiencing many

things for the first time, at the same time. There are new people, new noises, new smells and new things to investigate, so be gentle, be affectionate and be as comforting as you can be.

PUP'S FIRST NIGHT HOME

You have travelled home with your new charge safely in his crate. He's been to the vet for a thorough check-up; he's been weighed, his papers have been examined and perhaps he's even been vaccinated and wormed as well. He's met (and licked!) the whole family, including the excited children and the less-than-happy cat. He's explored his area, his new bed, the garden and anywhere else he's been permitted. He's eaten his first meal at home and relieved himself in the proper place. He's heard lots of new sounds, smelled new friends and seen more of the outside world than ever before...and that was just the first day! He's worn out and is ready for bed...or so you think!

QUALITY FOOD

The cost of food must be mentioned. All dogs need a good-quality food with an adequate supply of protein to develop their bones and muscles properly. Most dogs are not picky eaters but, unless fed properly, can quickly succumb to skin problems.

'YOU BETTER SHOP AROUND!'
Finding a reputable breeder who sells healthy pups is very important, but make sure that the breeder you choose is not only someone you respect but also someone with whom you feel comfortable. Your breeder will be a resource long after you buy your puppy, and you must be able to call with reasonable questions without being made to feel like a pest! If you don't connect on a personal level, investigate some other breeders before making a final decision.

It's puppy's first night home and you are ready to say 'Good night.' Keep in mind that this is his first night ever to be sleeping alone. His dam and littermates are no longer at paw's length and he's a bit scared, cold and lonely. Be reassuring to your new family member, but this is not the time to spoil him and give in to his inevitable whining.

Puppies whine. They whine to let others know where they are and hopefully to get company out of it. At bedtime, place your pup in his new bed or crate in his designated area and close the door. Mercifully, he may fall asleep without a peep. When the inevitable occurs, however, ignore the whining—he is fine. Be strong and keep his interest in mind. Do not allow yourself to feel guilty

and visit the pup. He will fall asleep eventually.

Many breeders recommend placing a piece of bedding from the pup's former home in his new bed so that he recognises and is comforted by the scent of his littermates. Others still advise placing a hot water bottle in the bed for warmth. The latter may be a good idea provided the pup doesn't attempt to suckle—he'll get good and wet, and may not fall asleep so fast.

Puppy's first night can be somewhat stressful for both the pup and his new family. Remember that you are setting the tone of night-time at your house. Unless you want to play with your pup every night at 10 p.m.,

It is your responsibility to clean up after your dog has relieved himself. You can purchase a tool to assist you in this task.

Every pup needs the opportunity to explore, so give your curious spaniel time to get acquainted with his new home, indoors and out, under your watchful eye.

pet and, in general, think is absolutely precious!

Besides getting to know his new family, your puppy should be exposed to other people, animals and situations. This will help him become well adjusted as he grows up and less prone to being timid or fearful of the new things he will encounter. Of course, he must not come into close contact with dogs you don't know well until his course of injections is fully complete.

Your pup's socialisation began with the breeder, but now it is your responsibility to continue it. The socialisation he receives until the age of 12 weeks is the most critical, as this is the time when he forms his impressions of the outside world. The eight-to-ten-week-old period is known as the fear period. The interaction he

midnight and 2 a.m., don't initiate the habit. Your family will thank you, and so will your pup!

PREVENTING PUPPY PROBLEMS

SOCIALISATION

Now that you have done all of the preparatory work and have helped your pup get accustomed to his new home and family, it is about time for you to have some fun! Socialising your King Charles Spaniel pup gives you the opportunity to show off your new friend, and your pup gets to reap the benefits of being an adorable furry creature that people will want to

PUPPY PROBLEMS

The majority of problems that are commonly seen in young pups will disappear as your dog gets older. However, how you deal with problems when he is young will determine how he reacts to discipline as an adult dog. It is important to establish who is boss (hopefully it will be you!) right away when you are first bonding with your dog. This bond will set the tone for the rest of your life together.

PUP MEETS WORLD

Thorough socialisation includes not only meeting new people but also being introduced to new experiences such as riding in the car, having his coat brushed, hearing the television, walking in a crowd—the list is endless. The more your pup experiences, and the more positive the experiences are, the less of a shock and the less frightening it will be for your pup to encounter new things.

receives during this time should be gentle and reassuring. Lack of socialisation, and/or negative experiences during the socialisation period, can manifest itself in fear and aggression as the dog grows up. Your puppy needs lots of positive interaction, which of course includes human contact, affection, handling and exposure to other animals.

Once your pup has received his necessary vaccinations, feel free to take him out and about (on his lead, of course). Walk him around the neighbourhood, take him on your daily errands, let people pet him, let him meet other dogs and pets, etc. Puppies do not have to try to make friends; there will be no shortage of people who will want to introduce themselves. Just make sure that you carefully supervise each meeting. If the neighbour-

hood children want to say hello, for example, that is great—children and pups most often make great companions. However, sometimes an excited child can unintentionally handle a pup too roughly, or an overzealous pup can playfully nip a little too hard.

SOCIALISATION PERIOD

The socialisation period for puppies is from age 8 to 16 weeks. This is the time when puppies need to leave their birth family and take up residence with their new owners, where they will meet many new people, other pets, etc. Failure to be adequately socialised can cause the dog to grow up fearing others and being shy and unfriendly due to a lack of self-confidence.

Socialisation begins at the breeder's, as littermates play with each other and learn the rules of the pack through their interactions.

You want to make socialisation experiences positive ones. What a pup learns during this very formative stage will affect his attitude toward future encounters. You want your dog to be comfortable around everyone. A pup that has a bad experience with a child may grow up to be a dog that is shy around or aggressive toward children.

CONSISTENCY IN TRAINING

Dogs, being pack animals, naturally need a leader, or else they try to establish dominance in their packs. When you welcome a dog into your family, the choice of who becomes the leader and who becomes the 'pack' is entirely up to you! Your pup's intuitive quest for dominance, coupled with the fact that it is nearly impossible to look at an adorable King Charles Spaniel pup with his 'puppy-dog'

eyes and not cave in, give the pup almost an unfair advantage in getting the upper hand! A pup will definitely test the waters to see what he can and cannot do. Do not give in to those pleading eyes—stand your ground when it comes to disciplining the pup and make sure that all family members do the same. It will only confuse the pup if Mother tells him to get off the sofa when he is used to sitting up there with Father to watch the nightly news. Avoid discrepancies by having all members of the household decide on the rules before the pup even comes home...and be consistent in enforcing them! Early training shapes the dog's personality, so you cannot be unclear in what you expect.

MANNERS MATTER

During the socialisation process, a puppy should meet people, experience different environments and definitely be exposed to other canines. Through playing and interacting with other dogs, your puppy will learn lessons, ranging from controlling the pressure of his jaws by biting his littermates to the inner-workings of the canine pack that he will apply to his human relationships for the rest of his life. That is why removing a puppy from its litter too early can be detrimental to the pup's development.

COMMON PUPPY PROBLEMS

The best way to prevent puppy problems is to be proactive in stopping an undesirable behaviour as soon as it starts. The old saying 'You can't teach an old dog new tricks' does not necessarily hold true, but it is true that it is much easier to discourage bad behaviour in a young developing pup than to wait until the pup's bad behaviour becomes the adult dog's bad habit. There are some problems that are especially prevalent in puppies as they develop.

NIPPING

As puppies start to teethe, they feel the need to sink their teeth into anything available...unfortunately, that usually includes your fingers, arms, hair and toes. You may find this behaviour cute for the first five seconds...until you feel just how sharp those puppy teeth are. Nipping is something you want to discourage immediately and consistently with a firm 'No!' (or whatever number of firm 'Nos' it takes for him to understand that you mean business). Then, replace your finger with an appropriate chew toy. While this behaviour is merely annoying when the dog is young, it can become dangerous as your King Charles Spaniel's adult teeth grow in and his jaws develop, and he continues to think it is okay to gnaw on human appendages. Your King Charles Spaniel does not mean any harm with a friendly nip, but he also does not know his own strength.

CRYING/WHINING

Your pup will often cry, whine, whimper, howl or make some type of commotion when he is left alone. This is basically his way of calling out for attention to make

A FORTNIGHT'S GRACE

It will take at least two weeks for your puppy to become accustomed to his new surroundings. Give him lots of love, attention, handling, frequent opportunities to relieve himself, a diet he likes to eat and a place he can call his own.

A soft, warm bed and toys to keep him occupied are among the things that will make your pup's transition to his new home as stress-free as possible.

sure that you know he is there and that you have not forgotten about him. Your puppy feels insecure when he is left alone, when you are out of the house and he is in his crate or when you are in another part of the house and he cannot see you. The noise he is making is an expression of the anxiety he feels at being alone, so he needs to be taught that being alone is okay. You are not actually training the dog to stop making noise; rather, you are training him to feel comfortable when he is alone and thus removing the need for him to make the noise.

This is where the crate with cosy bedding and a toy comes in handy. You want to know that your pup is safe when you are not there to supervise, and you know that he will be safe in his crate

rather than roaming freely about the house. In order for the pup to stay in his crate without making a fuss, he first needs to be comfortable in his crate. On that note, it is extremely important that the crate is never used as a form of punishment; this will cause the pup to view the crate as a negative place, rather than as a place of his own for safety and retreat.

Accustom the pup to the crate in short, gradually increasing time intervals in which you put him in the crate, maybe with a treat, and stay in the room with him. If he cries or makes a fuss, do not go to him, but stay in his sight. Gradually he will realise that staying in his crate is all right without your help, and it will not be so traumatic for him when you are not around. You may want to leave the radio on softly when you leave the house; the sound of human voices may be comforting to him.

TRAINING TIP

Training your puppy takes much patience and can be frustrating at times, but you should see results from your efforts. If you have a puppy that seems untrainable, take him to a trainer or behaviourist. The dog may have a personality problem that requires the help of a professional, or perhaps you need help in learning how to train your dog.

DIETARY AND FEEDING CONSIDERATIONS

Today the choices of food for your King Charles Spaniel are many and varied. There are simply dozens of brands of food in all sorts of flavours and textures, ranging from puppy diets to those for veterans. There are even hypoallergenic and low-calorie diets available. Because your King Charles Spaniel's food has a bearing on coat, health and temperament, it is essential that the most suitable diet is selected for a King Charles Spaniel of his age. It is fair to say, however, that even experienced owners can be perplexed by the enormous range of foods available. Only understanding what is best for your dog will help you reach an informed decision.

Dog foods are produced in three basic types: dried, semi-moist and tinned. Dried foods are useful for the cost-conscious, for overall they tend to be less expensive than semi-moist or tinned foods. Dried foods also contain the least fat and the most preservatives. In general, tinned foods are made up of 60–70 percent water, while semi-moist

FOOD STORAGE
You must store your dried dog food carefully. Open packages of dog food quickly lose their vitamin value, usually within 90 days of being opened. Mould spores and vermin could also contaminate open containers of food.

ones often contain so much sugar that they are perhaps the least preferred by owners, even though their dogs seem to like them.

FOOD PREFERENCE

Selecting the best dog food is difficult. There is no majority consensus among veterinary scientists as to the value of nutrient analyses (protein, fat, fibre, moisture, ash, cholesterol, minerals, etc.). All agree that feeding trials are what matter, but you also have to consider the individual dog. The dog's weight, age and activity level, and what pleases his taste, all must be considered. It is probably best to take the advice of your veterinary surgeon. Every dog's dietary requirements vary, even during the lifetime of a particular dog.

If your dog is fed a good dog food, it does not require supplements of meat or vegetables. Dogs do appreciate a little variety in their diets, so you may choose to stay with the same brand but vary the flavour. Alternatively, you may wish to add a little flavoured stock to give a difference to the taste.

When selecting your dog's diet, three stages of development must be considered: the puppy stage, the adult stage and the senior or veteran stage.

Puppy Stage

Puppies instinctively want to suck milk from their mother's teats; a normal puppy will exhibit this behaviour just a few moments following birth. If puppies do not attempt to suckle within the first half-hour or so, they should be encouraged to do so by placing them on the nipples, having selected ones with plenty of milk. This early milk supply is important in providing the essential colostrum, which protects the puppies during the first eight to ten weeks of their lives. Although a mother's milk is much better than any milk formula, despite there being some excellent ones available, if the puppies do not feed, the breeder will have to feed them by hand. For those with less experience, advice from a veterinary surgeon is important so that not only the right quantity of milk is fed but also that of correct quality, fed at suitably frequent intervals, usually every two hours during the first few days of life.

Puppies should be allowed to nurse from their mothers for about the first six weeks, although, starting around the third or fourth week, the breeder will begin to

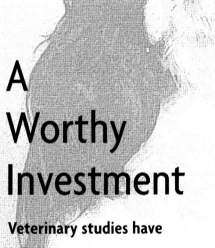

A Worthy Investment

Veterinary studies have proven that a balanced high-quality diet pays off in your dog's coat quality, behaviour and activity level. Invest in premium brands for the maximum payoff with your dog.

introduce small portions of suitable solid food. Most breeders like to introduce alternate milk and meat meals initially, building up to weaning time.

By the time the puppies are seven or a maximum of eight weeks old, they should be fully weaned and fed solely on a proprietary puppy food. Selection of the most suitable, good-quality diet at this time is essential, for a puppy's fastest growth rate is during the first year of life. Veterinary surgeons are usually able to offer advice in this regard and, although the frequency of meals will be reduced over time, only when a young dog has reached the age of about eight months should an adult diet be fed. Puppy and junior diets should be well balanced for the needs of your dog so that, except in certain circumstances, additional vitamins, minerals and proteins will not be required.

ADULT DIETS

A dog is considered an adult when it has stopped growing, so in general the diet of a King Charles Spaniel can be changed to an adult one at about eight months of age. Again you should rely upon your veterinary surgeon or dietary specialist to recommend an acceptable maintenance diet. Major dog-food manufacturers specialise in this type of food, and it is merely necessary for you to select the one best suited to your dog's needs. Active dogs may have different requirements from sedate dogs.

VETERAN DIETS

As dogs get older, their metabolism changes. The older dog usually exercises less, moves

---

THE CANINE GOURMET

Your dog does not prefer a fresh bone. Indeed, he wants it properly aged and, if given such a treat indoors, he is more likely to try to bury it in the carpet than he is to settle in for a good chew! If you have a garden, give him such delicacies outside and guide him to a place suitable for his 'bone yard.' He will carefully place the treasure in its earthy vault and seemingly forget about it. Trust me, his seeming distaste or lack of thanks for your thoughtfulness is not that at all. He will return in a few days to inspect the bone, perhaps to re-bury it, and, when it is just right, he will relish it as much as you do that cooked-to-perfection steak. If he is in a concrete or bricked kennel run, he will be especially frustrated at the hopelessness of the situation. He will vacillate between ignoring it completely, giving it a few licks to speed the curing process with saliva and trying to hide it behind the water bowl! When the bone has aged a bit, he will set to work on it.

Your breeder should provide you with a diet sheet, detailing exactly how and what your puppy has been fed. Take some of the puppy's food home with you when you acquire your puppy, and make any changes gradually to avoid stomach upset.

more slowly and sleeps more. This change in lifestyle and physiological performance requires a change in diet. Since these changes take place slowly, they might not be recognisable. What is easily recognisable is weight gain. By continuing to feed your dog an adult-maintenance diet when it is slowing down metabolically, your dog will gain weight. Obesity in an older dog compounds the health problems that already accompany old age.

FEEDING TIPS
- Dog food must be served at room temperature, neither too hot nor too cold. Fresh water, changed daily and served in a clean bowl, is mandatory, especially when feeding dried food.
- Never feed your dog from the table while you are eating, and never feed your dog leftovers from your own meal. They usually contain too much fat and too much seasoning.
- Dogs must chew their food. Hard pellets are excellent; soups and slurries are to be avoided.
- Don't add leftovers or any extras to normal dog food. The commercial food is usually balanced, and adding something extra destroys the balance.
- Except for age-related changes, dogs do not require dietary variations. They can be fed the same diet, day after day, without becoming bored or ill.

As your dog gets older, few of his organs function up to par. The kidneys slow down and the intestines become less efficient. These age-related factors are best handled with a change in diet and a change in feeding times to give smaller portions that are more easily digested. There is no single

GRAIN-BASED DIETS

Some less expensive dog foods are based on grains and other plant proteins. While these products may appear to be attractively priced, many breeders prefer a diet based on animal proteins and believe that they are more conducive to your dog's health. Many grain-based diets rely on soya protein, which may cause flatulence (passing gas).

There are many cases, however, when your dog might require a special diet. These special requirements should only be recommended by your veterinary surgeon.

'DOES THIS COLLAR MAKE ME LOOK FAT?'

While humans may obsess about how they look and how trim their bodies are, many people believe that extra weight on their dogs is a good thing. The truth is, pets should not be over- or under-weight, as both can lead to or signal sickness. In order to tell how fit your pet is, run your hands over his ribs. Are his ribs buried under a layer of fat or are they sticking out considerably? If your pet is within his normal weight range, you should be able to feel the ribs easily, but they should not protrude abnormally. If you stand above him, the outline of his body should resemble an hourglass. Some breeds do tend to be leaner while some are a bit stockier, but making sure your dog is the right weight for his breed certainly will contribute to his good health.

best diet for every older dog. While many dogs do well on light or senior diets, other dogs do better on puppy diets or other special premium diets such as lamb and rice. Be sensitive to your senior King Charles Spaniel's diet, as this will help control other problems that may arise with your old friend.

WATER

Just as your dog needs proper nutrition from his food, water is an essential 'nutrient' as well.

DRINK, DRANK, DRUNK—MAKE IT A DOUBLE

In both humans and dogs, as well as other living organisms, water forms the major part of nearly every body tissue. Naturally, we take water for granted, but without it, life as we know it would cease.

For dogs, water is needed to keep their bodies functioning biochemically. Additionally, water is needed to replace the water lost while panting. Unlike humans, who are able to sweat to dissipate heat, dogs must pant to cool down, thereby losing the vital water from their bodies needed to regulate their body temperatures. Humans lose electrolyte-containing products and other body-fluid components through sweating; dogs do not lose anything except water.

Water is essential always, but especially so when the weather is hot or humid or when your dog is exercising or working vigorously.

Water keeps the dog's body properly hydrated and promotes normal function of the body's systems. During house-training, it is necessary to keep an eye on how much water your King Charles Spaniel is drinking, but once he is reliably trained he should have access to clean fresh water at all times, especially if you feed dried food. Make certain that the dog's water bowl is clean, and change the water often.

CHANGE IN DIET

As your dog's caretaker, you know the importance of keeping his diet consistent, but sometimes when you run out of food or if you're on holiday, you have to make a change quickly. Some dogs will experience digestive problems, but most will not. If you are planning on changing your dog's menu, do so gradually to ensure that your dog will not have any problems. Over a period of four to five days, slowly add some new food to your dog's old food, increasing the percentage of new food each day.

EXERCISE

It's fair to say that the King Charles Spaniel requires less exercise than all of the other spaniels! Toy dogs, by and small, are more prone to sitting on laps than running them. Nevertheless, some form of exercise is a basic requirement of life. A sedentary lifestyle is as harmful to a dog as it is to a person.

Given the breed's short legs and delicate structure, the King Charles Spaniel gets a good bit of his exercise moving around the home and garden. Yet, a nice walk outdoors on lead is enjoyable and healthy for both of you. Brisk walks, once the puppy reaches three or four months of age, will

EXERCISE ALERT!

You should be careful where you exercise your dog. Many countryside areas have been sprayed with chemicals that are highly toxic to both dogs and humans. Never allow your dog to eat grass or drink from puddles on either public or private grounds, as the run-off water may contain chemicals from sprays and herbicides.

the King Charles Spaniel. Fetching games can be played indoors or out; these are excellent for giving your dog active play that he will enjoy. Chasing things that move comes naturally to dogs of all breeds, especially spaniels. When your King Charles Spaniel runs after the ball or object, praise him for picking it up and encourage him to bring it back to you for another throw. Never go to the object and pick it up yourself, or you'll soon find that you are the one retrieving the objects rather than the dog! If you choose to play games outdoors, you must have a securely fenced-in garden and/or have the dog attached to at least an 8-metre (25-foot) light line for security. You want your King Charles Spaniel to run, but not run away!

Bear in mind that an overweight dog should never be suddenly over-exercised; instead he should be encouraged to increase exercise slowly. Not only is exercise essential to keep the dog's body fit, it is essential to his

stimulate heart rates and build muscle for both dog and owner. As the dog reaches adulthood, the speed and distance of the walks can be increased as long as they are kept reasonable and comfortable for both of you.

Play sessions in the garden and letting the dog run free in the garden under your supervision also are good forms of exercise for

EXERCISE CAUTION

Never tie a dog out to a post or tree, thinking that you are giving him exercise. This will only serve to increase aggression in the dog, The King Charles is not an aggressive breed by nature, but tying the dog out can cause him to act aggressively.

THAT'S ENTERTAINMENT!

Is your dog home alone for much of the day? If you haven't taught him how to crochet or play the French horn, then he'll probably need something to occupy his paws and jaws, lest he turn to chewing up the carpet and draperies. Recommended conditioning devices are toys that stimulate your dog both physically and mentally. Some of the most popular toys are those that are constructed to hide food inside. They provide not only a challenge but also instant gratification when your dog gets to the treat. Be sure to clean these carefully to prevent bacteria from building up.

mental well-being. A bored dog will find something to do, which often manifests itself in some type of destructive behaviour. In this sense, exercise is essential for the owner's mental well-being as well!

GROOMING YOUR KING CHARLES SPANIEL

Do understand before purchasing your dog that this is a breed with a coat that needs maintenance, although, fortunately, the King Charles is quite low-maintenance compared to most of the other toy breeds. Grooming is a must, whether you have a dog for the show ring or one that is an household pet. Think of it in

terms of your child—you bath your youngster, comb his hair and put a clean set of clothes on him. The end product is that you have a child that smells good and looks nice, and that you enjoy having in your company. It is the same with your King Charles—keep the dog brushed, combed and cleaned,

LET THE SUN SHINE

Your dog needs daily sunshine for the same reason people do. Pets kept inside homes with curtains drawn against the sun suffer from 'SAD' (Seasonal Affected Disorder) to the same degree as humans. We now know that sunlight must enter the iris and thus progress to the pineal gland to regulate the body's hormonal system. When we live and work in artificial light, both circadian rhythms and hormonal balances are disturbed.

Your local pet shop should carry all of the grooming tools that you'll need for maintaining your King Charles Spaniel's coat in peak condition.

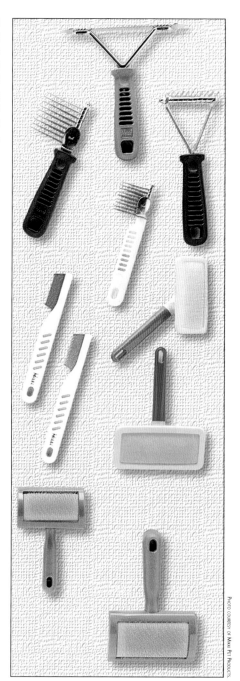

PHOTO COURTESY OF MIKKI PET PRODUCTS.

and you will find it a pleasure to be in his company.

Grooming is very fundamental with this breed. Despite their long coats, King Charles are more-or-less 'wash-and-go' dogs, although special care must be taken to keep the coat mat-free. The long feathering is most prone to mats and tangles; this includes the ears and ear area, the 'arm-pits,' the backs of the legs and the tail and surrounding area. Routine grooming should consist of a weekly brushing and combing, and bathing as needed, which will be probably about every few weeks. If you encounter a mat in the coat, try to separate it gently with your fingers. In the worst cases, you may need to cut the mat out, but it is better for the coat to untangle it yourself. Be gentle when combing through the feathering; the areas most prone to mats are also the most sensitive, and you do not want grooming to be a painful experience for your King Charles. This is not a breed that should be trimmed, although you should cut away excess hair between the toes and you may want to trim around the genital area for cleanliness.

Of course, you can eliminate all of the grooming for yourself, except for the weekly brushing, if you take your dog to the groomer every three months. However, many pet owners like to spend the time with their pets and, do

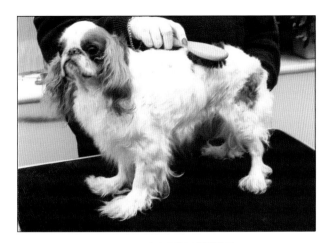

SOAP IT UP

The use of human soap products like shampoo, bubble bath and hand soap can be damaging to a dog's coat and skin. Human products are too strong; they remove the protective oils coating the dog's hair and skin that make him water-resistant. Use only shampoo made especially for dogs. You may like to use a medicated shampoo, which will help to keep external parasites at bay.

remember, many pet owners do a much better job grooming their dogs than some professional groomers.

With routine grooming, you will have an happy, clean and good-smelling King Charles Spaniel who will look nice and tidy, and whom you will be happy to take out in public.

BATHING

Dogs do not need to be bathed as often as humans, but regular bathing is essential for healthy skin and an healthy, shiny coat. Again, like most anything, if you accustom your pup to being bathed as a puppy, it will be second nature by the time he grows up. You want your dog to be at ease in the bath or else it could end up a wet, soapy, messy ordeal for both of you!

Brush your King Charles Spaniel thoroughly before wetting

Above: Use a grooming table with a non-skid surface, adjusted to a proper height. A bristle brush can be used on the body coat. Left: A fine-toothed comb can be used gently on the long ear feathering.

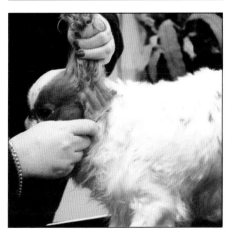

Don't forget under the ears. Out-of-the-way areas tend to mat more easily and are more sensitive, so always use a gentle touch.

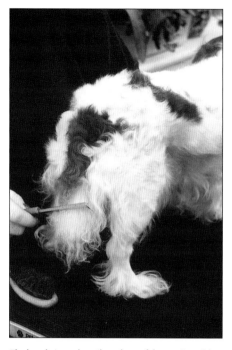

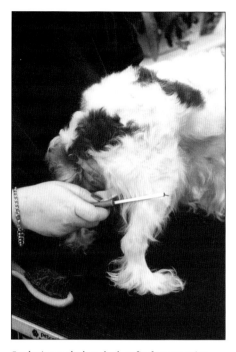

The long hair on the tail needs careful attention with the comb, as it can become tangled easily.

Feathering on the legs also benefits from attention with the fine-toothed comb.

Tear stains and dirt around the eyes can be removed easily with a soft wipe and a cleanser made for this purpose.

Use grooming time to clean the dog's ears, using an ear powder made for dogs and being careful to never probe into the ear canal.

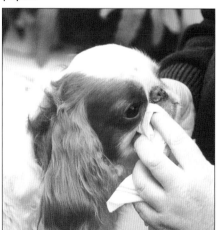

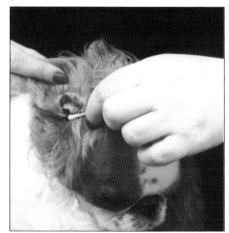

BATHING BEAUTY

Once you are sure that the dog is thoroughly rinsed, squeeze the excess water out of his coat with your hand and dry him with an heavy towel until fairly dry. You may choose to use a blaster on his coat to finish the job. Be sure to brush thoroughly after drying. In cold weather, never allow your dog outside with a wet coat.

There are 'dry bath' products on the market, which are sprays and powders intended for spot cleaning that can be used between regular baths if necessary. They are not substitutes for regular baths, but they are easy to use for touch-ups as they do not require rinsing.

his coat. This will get rid of most mats and tangles, which are harder to remove when the coat is wet. Make certain that your dog has a good non-slip surface on which to stand. Begin by wetting the dog's coat, checking the water temperature to make sure that it is neither too hot nor too cold. A shower or hose attachment is necessary for thoroughly wetting and rinsing the coat.

Next, apply shampoo to the dog's coat and work it into a good lather. Wash the head last, as you do not want shampoo to drip into the dog's eyes while you are washing the rest of his body. You should use only a shampoo that is made for dogs. Do not use a

product made for human hair. Work the shampoo all the way down to the skin. You can use this opportunity to check the skin for any bumps, bites or other abnormalities. Do not neglect any area of the body—get all of the hard-to-reach places.

Once the dog has been thoroughly shampooed, he requires an equally thorough rinsing. Shampoo left in the coat can be irritating to the dog's skin. Protect his eyes from the shampoo by shielding them with your hand and directing the flow of water in the opposite direction. You also should avoid getting water in the ear canal. Be prepared for your dog to shake out his coat—you might want to stand back, but make sure you have an hold on the dog to keep him from running through the house.

Ear Cleaning

The King Charles's pendulous ears should be kept clean with a cotton wipe and ear powder made especially for dogs. Do not probe into the ear canal with a cotton bud, as this can cause injury. Be on the lookout for any signs of infection or ear-mite infestation. If your King Charles Spaniel has been shaking his head or scratching at his ears frequently, this usually indicates a problem. If the dog's ears have an unusual odour, this is a sure sign of mite infestation or infection, and a

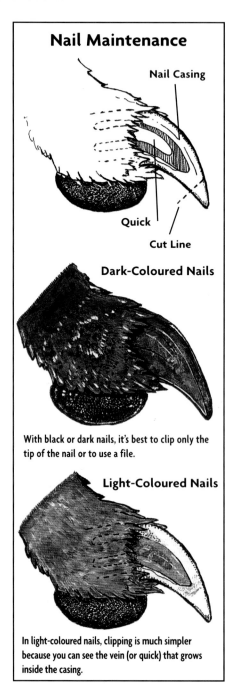

Nail Maintenance

Nail Casing

Quick

Cut Line

Dark-Coloured Nails

With black or dark nails, it's best to clip only the tip of the nail or to use a file.

Light-Coloured Nails

In light-coloured nails, clipping is much simpler because you can see the vein (or quick) that grows inside the casing.

signal to have his ears checked by the veterinary surgeon.

NAIL CLIPPING

Your King Charles Spaniel should be accustomed to having his nails trimmed at an early age since nail clipping will be part of your maintenance routine throughout his life. Not only does it look nicer, but long nails can scratch someone unintentionally. Also, a long nail has a better chance of ripping and bleeding, or of causing the feet to spread. A good rule of thumb is that if you can hear your dog's nails' clicking on the floor when he walks, his nails are too long.

Before you start cutting, make sure you can identify the 'quick' in each nail. The quick is a blood vessel that runs through the centre of each nail and grows rather close to the end. The quick will bleed if accidentally cut, which will be quite painful for the dog as it contains nerve endings. Keep some type of clotting agent on hand, such as a styptic pencil or styptic powder (the type used for shaving). This will stop the bleeding quickly when applied to the end of the cut nail. Do not panic if you cut the quick, just stop the bleeding and talk soothingly to your dog. Once he has calmed down, move on to the next nail. It is better to clip a little at a time, particularly with black-nailed dogs.

NAIL FILING

You can purchase an electric tool to grind down a dog's nails rather than cut them. Some dogs don't seem to mind the electric grinder but will object strongly to nail clippers. Talking it over with your veterinary surgeon will help you make the right choice.

Your pet shop sells different styles of nail clippers. Select a sturdy, efficient one for your King Charles.

Hold your pup steady as you begin trimming his nails; you do not want him to make any sudden movements or run away. Talk to him soothingly and stroke him as you clip. Holding his foot in your hand, simply take off the end of each nail with one swift clip. You should purchase nail clippers that are made for use on dogs; you can probably find them wherever you buy pet or grooming supplies.

TRAVELLING WITH YOUR DOG

CAR TRAVEL

You should accustom your King Charles Spaniel to riding in a car at an early age. You may or may not take him in the car often, but at the very least he will need to go to the vet and you do not want these trips to be traumatic for the dog or troublesome for you. The safest way for a dog to ride in the car is in his crate. If he uses a crate in the house, you can use the same crate for travel.

Put the pup in the crate and see how he reacts. If he seems uneasy, you can have a passenger hold him on his lap while you drive. Another option for car travel is a specially made safety harness for dogs, which straps the dog in much like a seat belt. Do not let the dog roam loose in the vehicle—this is very dangerous! If you should stop short, your dog can be thrown and injured. If the dog starts climbing on you and pestering you while you are driving, you will not be able to concentrate on the road. It is an unsafe situation for everyone—human and canine.

For long trips, be prepared to stop to let the dog relieve himself. Take with you whatever you need

ON THE ROAD

If you are going on a long motor trip with your dog, be sure the hotels are dog-friendly. Many hotels do not accept dogs. Also take along some ice that can be thawed and offered to your dog if he becomes overheated. Most dogs like to lick ice, and it will help him to cool off.

to clean up after him, including some paper kitchen towels and perhaps some old towelling for use should he have a toileting accident in the car or suffer from travel sickness.

AIR TRAVEL

While it is possible to take a dog on a flight within Britain, this is fairly unusual and advance permission is always required. The dog will be required to travel in a fibreglass crate. Many toy dogs are small enough to be carried on and can travel in the cabin, in their crates with their owners. You should always check in advance with the airline regarding specific rules and requirements.

To help put the dog at ease, give him one of his favourite toys in the crate. Do not feed the dog for at least six hours before checking in, in order to minimise his need to relieve himself. However, certain regulations specify that water must always be made available to the dog in the crate.

Make sure your dog is properly identified and that your contact information appears on his ID tags and on his crate. Every rule must be strictly followed so as to prevent the risk of getting separated from your dog.

Locate a kennel convenient to your home. Be sure that the facilities are immaculately kept and professionally run, particularly by people with experience in toy dogs.

BOARDING AND HOLIDAYS

So you want to take a family holiday—and you want to include *all* members of the family. You would probably make arrangements for accommodation ahead of time anyway, but this is especially important when travelling with a dog. You do not want to make an overnight stop at the only place around for miles, only to find out that they do not allow dogs. Also, you do not want to reserve a place for your family without confirming that you are travelling with a dog, because, if it is against their policy, you may end up without a place to stay.

Alternatively, if you are travelling and choose not to bring your King Charles Spaniel, you will have to make arrangements for him while you are away. Some options are to take him to a neighbour's house to stay while you are gone, to have a trusted neighbour pop in often or stay at your house or to bring your dog to a reputable boarding kennel. If you choose to board him at a kennel, you should visit in advance to see the facilities provided and where the dogs are kept. Are the dogs' areas spacious and kept clean? Talk to some of the employees and see how they treat the dogs—do they spend time with the dogs, play with them, exercise them, etc.? Also find out the kennel's policy on vaccinations and what they

No dog should ever be allowed outdoors without his collar and ID tags.

require. This is for all of the dogs' safety, since there is a greater risk of diseases being passed from dog to dog when dogs are kept together.

IDENTIFICATION

Your King Charles Spaniel is your valued companion and friend. That is why you always keep a close eye on him and you have made sure that he cannot escape from the garden or wriggle out of his collar and run away from you. However, accidents can happen and there may come a time when your dog unexpectedly becomes separated from you. If this unfortunate event should occur, the first thing on your mind will be finding him. Proper identification, including an ID tag, a tattoo and possibly a microchip, will increase the chances of his being returned to you safely and quickly.

Living with an untrained dog is a lot like owning a piano that you do not know how to play—it is a nice object to look at, but it does not do much more than that to bring you pleasure. Now try taking piano lessons, and suddenly the piano comes alive and brings forth magical sounds and rhythms that set your heart singing and your body swaying.

The same is true with your King Charles Spaniel. Any dog is a big responsibility and, if not trained sensibly, may develop unacceptable behaviour that annoys you or could even cause family friction.

To train your King Charles Spaniel, you may like to enrol in

Perhaps the biggest challenge in training a pup is getting his attention. A tasty titbit is a sure way to get him to focus and to associate training with fun.

> **PARENTAL GUIDANCE**
> Training a dog is a life experience. Many parents admit that much of what they know about raising children they learned from caring for their dogs. Dogs respond to love, fairness and guidance, just as children do. Become a good dog owner and you may become an even better parent.

an obedience class. Teach your dog good manners as you learn how and why he behaves the way he does. Find out how to communicate with your dog and how to recognise and understand his communications with you. Suddenly the dog takes on a new role in your life—he is clever, interesting, well behaved and fun to be with. He demonstrates his bond of devotion to you daily. In other words, your King Charles Spaniel does wonders for your ego because he constantly reminds you that you are not only his leader, you are his hero!

Those involved with teaching dog obedience and counselling owners about their dogs' behaviour have discovered some interesting facts about dog ownership. For example, training dogs when they are puppies results in the highest rate of success in developing well-mannered and well-adjusted adult dogs. Training an older dog, from six months to six years of age, can produce almost equal results, providing that the owner accepts the dog's slower rate of learning capability and is willing to work patiently to help the dog succeed at developing to his fullest potential. Unfortunately, many owners of untrained adult dogs lack the patience factor, so they do not persist until their dogs are successful at learning particular behaviours.

Training a puppy aged 10 to 16 weeks (20 weeks at the most) is like working with a dry sponge in a pool of water. The pup soaks up whatever you show him and constantly looks for more things to do and learn. At this early age, his body is not yet producing hormones, and therein lies the reason for such an high rate of success. Without hormones, he is focused on his owners and not particularly interested in investigating other places, dogs, people, etc. You are his leader: his provider of food, water, shelter and security. He latches onto you and wants to stay close. He will usually follow you from room to room, will not let you out of his

HONOUR AND OBEY

Dogs are the most honourable animals in existence. They consider another species (humans) as their own. They interface with you. You are their leader. King Charles perceive children to be on their level; their actions around small children are different from their behaviour around their adult masters.

It's a big world to a small King Charles puppy! Your pup needs your guidance and training to ensure his safety.

sight when you are outdoors with him and will respond in like manner to the people and animals you encounter. If you greet a friend warmly, he will be happy to greet the person as well. If, however, you are hesitant or anxious about the approach of a stranger, he will respond accordingly.

Once the puppy begins to produce hormones, his natural curiosity emerges and he begins to investigate the world around him. It is at this time when you may notice that the untrained dog begins to wander away from you and even ignore your commands to stay close. When this behaviour becomes a problem, you have two choices: get rid of the dog or train him. It is strongly urged that you choose the latter option.

You usually will be able to find obedience classes within a reasonable distance from your home, but you can also do a lot to train your dog yourself. Sometimes there are classes available, but the tuition is too costly. Whatever the circumstances, the solution to training your dog without obedience classes lies within the pages of this book.

This chapter is devoted to helping you train your King Charles Spaniel at home. If the recommended procedures are followed faithfully, you may expect positive results that will

THE HAND THAT FEEDS

To a dog's way of thinking, your hands are like his mouth in terms of a defence mechanism. If you squeeze him too tightly, he might just bite you because that would be his normal response. This is not aggressive biting and, although all biting should be discouraged, you need the discipline in learning how to handle your dog.

prove rewarding both to you and your dog.

Whether your new charge is a puppy or a mature adult, the methods of teaching and the techniques we use in training basic behaviours are the same. After all, no dog, whether puppy or adult, likes harsh or inhumane methods. All creatures, however, respond favourably to gentle motivational methods and sincere praise and encouragement. Now let us get started.

HOUSE-TRAINING

You can train a puppy to relieve himself wherever you choose, but this must be somewhere suitable. You should bear in mind from the outset that when your puppy is old enough to go out in public places, any canine deposits must be removed at once. You will always have to carry with you a small plastic bag or 'poop-scoop.'

Outdoor training includes

REAP THE REWARDS

If you start with a normal, healthy dog and give him time, patience and some carefully executed lessons, you will reap the rewards of that training for the life of the dog. And what a life it will be! The two of you will find immeasurable pleasure in the companionship you have built together with love, respect and understanding.

such surfaces as grass, soil and cement. Indoor training usually means training your dog to newspaper. When deciding on the surface and location that you will want your King Charles Spaniel to use, be sure it is going to be permanent. Training your dog to grass and then changing your mind a few months later is extremely difficult for both dog and owner.

Next, choose the command you will use each and every time you want your puppy to void. 'Hurry up' and 'Toilet' are examples of commands commonly used by dog owners. Get in the habit of giving the puppy your chosen relief command before you take him out. That way, when he becomes an adult, you will be able to determine if he wants to go out when you ask him. A confirmation will be signs of interest, such as wagging his tail, watching you intently, going to the door, etc.

PUPPY'S NEEDS

Puppy needs to relieve himself after play periods, after each meal, after he has been sleeping and at any time he indicates that he is looking for a place to urinate or defecate. The urinary and intestinal tract muscles of very young puppies are not fully developed. Therefore, like human babies, puppies need to relieve themselves frequently.

Take your puppy out often—every hour for an eight-week-old, for example—and always immediately after sleeping and eating. The older the puppy, the less often he will need to relieve himself. Finally, as a mature healthy adult, he will require only three to five relief trips per day.

HOUSING

Since the types of housing and control you provide for your puppy have a direct relationship on the success of house-training, we consider the various aspects of both before we begin training.

Taking a new puppy home and turning him loose in your house can be compared to turning a child loose in a sports arena and telling the child that the place is all his! The sheer enormity of the place would be too much for him to handle. Instead, offer the puppy clearly defined areas where he can play, sleep, eat and live. A room of the house where the family gathers is the most obvious choice. Puppies are social animals and need to feel a part of the pack right from the start. Hearing your voice, watching you while you are doing things and smelling you nearby are all positive reinforcers that he is now a member of your pack. Usually a family room, the kitchen or a nearby adjoining breakfast area is ideal for providing safety and security for both puppy and owner.

THINK BEFORE YOU BARK

Dogs are sensitive to their masters' moods and emotions. Use your voice wisely when communicating with your dog. Never raise your voice at your dog unless you are angry and trying to correct him. 'Barking' at your dog can become as meaningless as 'dogspeak' is to you.

Within the designated room, there should be a smaller area that the puppy can call his own. An alcove, a wire or fibreglass dog crate or a fenced (not boarded!) corner from which he can view the activities of his new family will be fine. The size of the area or crate is the key factor here. The area must be large enough so that the puppy can lie down and stretch out, as well as stand up,

PAPER CAPER

Never line your pup's sleeping area with newspaper. Puppy litters are usually raised on newspaper and, once in your home, the puppy will immediately associate newspaper with voiding. Never put newspaper on any floor while house-training, as this will only confuse the puppy. If you are paper-training him, use paper in his designated relief area ONLY. Finally, restrict water intake after evening meals. Offer a few licks at a time—never let a young puppy gulp water after meals.

remain close to their relief areas unless forced to do so. In those cases, they then become dirty dogs and usually remain that way for life.

The dog's designated area should contain clean bedding and a toy. Water must always be available, in a non-spill container, once house-training has been achieved reliably.

CONTROL

By control, we mean helping the puppy to create a lifestyle pattern that will be compatible to that of his human pack (YOU!). Just as we guide little children to learn our way of life, we must show the puppy when it is time to play, eat, sleep, exercise and even entertain himself.

Your puppy should always sleep in his crate. He should also learn that, during times of household confusion and excessive human activity, such as at breakfast when family members are preparing for the day, he can play by himself in relative safety and comfort in his designated area. Each time you leave the puppy alone, he should understand exactly where he is to stay.

Puppies usually enjoy chewing on just about anything. They cannot tell the difference between lamp and television leads, shoes, table legs, etc. Chewing into a television lead, for

without rubbing his head on the top. At the same time, it must be small enough so that he cannot relieve himself at one end and sleep at the other without coming into contact with his droppings before he is fully trained to relieve himself outside. Dogs are, by nature, clean animals and will not

CANINE DEVELOPMENT TIMETABLE

It is important to understand how and at what age a puppy develops into adulthood.
If you are a puppy owner, consult the following Canine Development Timetable to
determine the stage of development your puppy is currently experiencing.
This knowledge will help you as you work with the puppy in the weeks and months ahead.

Period	Age	Characteristics
FIRST TO THIRD	BIRTH TO SEVEN WEEKS	Puppy needs food, sleep and warmth, and responds to simple and gentle touching. Needs mother for security and disciplining. Needs littermates for learning and interacting with other dogs. Pup learns to function within a pack and learns pack order of dominance. Begin socialising with adults and children for short periods. Begins to become aware of its environment.
FOURTH	EIGHT TO TWELVE WEEKS	Brain is fully developed. Needs socialising with outside world. Remove from mother and littermates. Needs to change from canine pack to human pack. Human dominance necessary. Fear period occurs between 8 and 12 weeks. Avoid fright and pain.
FIFTH	THIRTEEN TO SIXTEEN WEEKS	Training and formal obedience should begin. Less association with other dogs, more with people, places, situations. Period will pass easily if you remember this is pup's change-to-adolescence time. Be firm and fair. Flight instinct prominent. Permissiveness and over-disciplining can do permanent damage. Praise for good behaviour.
JUVENILE	FOUR TO EIGHT MONTHS	Another fear period about 7 to 8 months of age. It passes quickly, but be cautious of fright and pain. Sexual maturity reached. Dominant traits established. Dog should understand sit, down, come and stay by now.

NOTE: THESE ARE APPROXIMATE TIME FRAMES. ALLOW FOR INDIVIDUAL DIFFERENCES IN PUPPIES.

PRACTICE MAKES PERFECT!

- Have training lessons with your dog every day in several short segments—three to five times a day for a few minutes at a time is ideal.
- Do not have long practice sessions. The dog will become easily bored.
- Never practise when you are tired, ill, worried or in an otherwise negative mood. This will transmit to the dog and may have an adverse effect on his performance.

Think fun, short and above all POSITIVE! End each session on an high note, rather than a failed exercise, and make sure to give a lot of praise. Enjoy the training and help your dog enjoy it, too.

example, can be fatal to the puppy, while a shorted wire can start a fire in the house. If the puppy chews on the arm of the chair when he is alone, you will probably discipline him angrily when you get home. Thus, he makes the association that your coming home means he is going to be punished. (He will not remember chewing the chair and is incapable of making the association of the discipline with his naughty deed.) Accustoming the pup to his designated area not only keeps him safe but also avoids his engaging in destructive behaviours when you are not around.

Times of excitement, such as special occasions, family parties,

etc., can be fun for the puppy, providing that he can view the activities from the security of his designated area. He is not underfoot and he is not being fed all sorts of titbits that will probably cause him stomach distress, yet he still feels a part of the fun.

TOILETING TIMETABLE

A puppy should be taken to his relief area each time he is released from his designated area, after meals, after a play session and when he first awakens in the morning (at age eight weeks, this can mean 5 a.m.!). The puppy will indicate that he's ready 'to go' by circling or sniffing busily—do not misinterpret these signs. For a puppy less than ten weeks of age, a routine of taking him out every hour is necessary. As the puppy grows, he will be able to wait for

MEALTIME

Mealtime should be a peaceful time for your puppy. Do not put his food and water bowls in an high-traffic area in the house. For example, give him his own little corner of the kitchen where he can eat undisturbed and where he will not be underfoot. Do not allow small children or other family members to disturb the pup when he is eating.

HOUSE-TRAINING TIP

Most of all, be consistent. Always take your dog to the same location, always use the same command and always have the dog on lead when he is in his relief area, unless a fenced-in garden is available.

By following the Success Method, your puppy will be completely house-trained by the time his muscle and brain development reach maturity. Keep in mind that small breeds usually mature faster than large breeds, but all puppies should be trained by six months of age.

longer periods of time.

Keep trips to his relief area short. Stay no more than five or six minutes and then return to the house. If he goes during that time, praise him lavishly and take him indoors immediately. If he does not, but he has an accident when you go back indoors, pick him up immediately, say 'No! No!' and

TAKE THE LEAD

Do not carry your dog to his toilet area. Lead him there on a leash or, better yet, encourage him to follow you to the spot. If you start carrying him to his spot, you might end up doing this routine forever and your dog will have the satisfaction of having trained YOU.

return to his relief area. Wait a few minutes, then return to the house again. Never hit a puppy or rub his face in urine or excrement when he has had an accident!

Once indoors, put the puppy in his crate until you have had time to clean up his accident. Then, release him to the family area and watch him more closely than before. Chances are, his accident was a result of your not

THE CLEAN LIFE

By providing sleeping and resting quarters that fit the dog, and offering frequent opportunities to relieve himself outside his quarters, the puppy quickly learns that the outdoors (or the newspaper if you are training him to paper) is the place to go when he needs to urinate or defecate. It also reinforces his innate desire to keep his sleeping quarters clean. This, in turn, helps develop the muscle control that will eventually produce a dog with clean living habits.

picking up his signal or waiting too long before offering him the opportunity to relieve himself. Never hold a grudge against the puppy for accidents.

Let the puppy learn that going outdoors means it is time to relieve himself, not to play. Once trained, he will be able to play indoors and out and still differentiate between the times for play versus the times for relief.

Help him develop regular hours for naps, being alone, playing by himself and just resting, all in his crate. Encourage him to entertain himself while you are busy with your activities. Let him learn that having you near is comforting, but it is not your main purpose in life to provide him with your undivided attention.

Each time you put your puppy in his own area, use the same command, whatever suits best. Soon he will run to his crate or special area when he hears you say those words.

Crate training provides safety for you, the puppy and the home. It also provides the puppy with a feeling of security, and that helps the puppy achieve self-confidence and clean habits. Remember that one of the primary ingredients in

THE SUCCESS METHOD

6 Steps to Successful Crate Training

1 Tell the puppy 'Crate time!' and place him in the crate with a small treat (a piece of cheese or half of a biscuit). Let him stay in the crate for five minutes while you are in the same room. Then release him and praise lavishly. Never release him when he is fussing. Wait until he is quiet before you let him out.

2 Repeat Step 1 several times a day.

3 The next day, place the puppy in the crate as before. Let him stay there for ten minutes. Do this several times.

4 Continue building time in five-minute increments until the puppy stays in his crate for 30 minutes with you in the room. Always take him to his relief area after prolonged periods in his crate.

5 Now go back to Step 1 and let the puppy stay in his crate for five minutes, this time while you are out of the room.

6 Once again, build crate time in five-minute increments with you out of the room. When the puppy will stay willingly in his crate (he may even fall asleep!) for 30 minutes with you out of the room, he will be ready to stay in it for several hours at a time.

THE SUCCESS METHOD

Success that comes by luck is usually short-lived. Success that comes by well-thought-out proven methods is often more easily achieved and permanent. This is the Success Method. It is designed to give you, the puppy owner, a simple yet proven way to help your puppy develop clean living habits and a feeling of security in his new environment.

house-training your puppy is control. Regardless of your lifestyle, there will always be occasions when you will need to have a place where your dog can stay and be happy and safe. Crate training is the answer for now and in the future.

In conclusion, a few key elements are really all you need

for a successful house-training method—consistency, frequency, praise, control and supervision. By following these procedures with a normal, healthy puppy, you and the puppy will soon be past the stage of 'accidents' and ready to move on to a full and rewarding life together.

Training your King Charles puppy ensures that your dog will be a delightful companion and a joy to have in the home.

HOW MANY TIMES A DAY?

AGE	RELIEF TRIPS
To 14 weeks	10
14–22 weeks	8
22–32 weeks	6
Adulthood	4
(dog stops growing)	

These are estimates, of course, but they are a guide to the number of opportunities a dog should have each day to relieve itself.

ROLES OF DISCIPLINE, REWARD AND PUNISHMENT

Discipline, training one to act in accordance with rules, brings order to life. It is as simple as that. Without discipline, particularly in a group society, chaos will reign supreme and the group will eventually perish. Humans and canines are social animals and need some form of discipline in order to function effectively. They must procure food, protect their home base and their young and reproduce to keep their species going. If there were no discipline

Training involves teaching the house rules in addition to the basic commands. Will your King Charles be allowed to join you on the sofa? Make a decision and enforce it consistently from puppyhood.

to be repeated. A behaviour that results in an unpleasant event tends not to be repeated. It is this theory upon which training methods are based today. For example, if you manipulate a dog to perform a specific behaviour and reward him for doing it, he is likely to do it again because he enjoyed the end result.

Occasionally, punishment, a penalty inflicted for an offence, is necessary. The best type of punishment often comes from an outside source. For example, a child is told not to touch the cooker because he may get burned. He disobeys and touches the cooker. In doing so, he receives a burn. From that time on, he respects the heat of the cooker and avoids contact with

in the lives of social animals, they would eventually die from starvation and/or predation by other stronger animals.

In the case of domestic canines, discipline in their lives is needed in order for them to understand how their pack (you and other family members) functions and how they must act in order to survive.

A large humane society in an highly populated area recently surveyed dog owners regarding their satisfaction with their relationships with their dogs. People who had trained their dogs were 75% more satisfied with their pets than those who had never trained their dogs.

Dr Edward Thorndike, a psychologist, established *Thorndike's Theory of Learning*, which states that a behaviour that results in a pleasant event tends

PLAN TO PLAY

The puppy should also have regular play and exercise sessions when he is with you or a family member. Exercise for a very young puppy can consist of a short walk around the house or garden. Playing can include fetching games with a ball or a special raggy. (All puppies teethe and need soft things upon which to chew.) Remember to restrict play periods to indoors within his living area (the family room, for example) until he is completely house-trained.

it. Therefore, a behaviour that results in an unpleasant event tends not to be repeated.

A good example of a dog's learning the hard way is the dog who chases the house cat. He is told many times to leave the cat alone, yet he persists in teasing the cat. Then, one day, the dog begins chasing the cat but the cat turns and swipes a claw across the dog's face, leaving the dog with a painful gash on his nose. The final result is that the dog stops chasing the cat. Again, a behaviour that results in an unpleasant event tends not to be repeated.

TRAINING EQUIPMENT

COLLAR AND LEAD

For a King Charles Spaniel, the collar and lead that you use for training must be one with which you are easily able to work, not too heavy for the dog and perfectly safe.

TREATS

Have a bag of treats on hand; something nutritious and easy to swallow works best. Use a soft treat, a chunk of cheese or a piece of cooked chicken rather than a dry biscuit. By the time the dog has finished chewing a dry treat,

Introductions between pets should be supervised so that no trouble arises from surprise meetings. Chances are, these two will grow up together being the best of friends.

Ensure that your King Charles' collar has a proper fit so that it will stay on the dog and be comfortable for him to wear.

he will forget why he is being rewarded in the first place!

Using food rewards will not teach a dog to beg at the table— the only way to teach a dog to beg at the table is to give him food from the table. In training, rewarding the dog with a food treat will help him associate praise and the treats with learning new behaviours that obviously please his owner.

TRAINING BEGINS: ASK THE DOG A QUESTION

In order to teach your dog anything, you must first get his attention. After all, he cannot learn anything if he is looking away from you with his mind on something else.

To get your dog's attention, ask him 'School?' and immediately walk over to him and give him a treat as you tell him 'Good dog.' Wait a minute or two and repeat the routine, this time with a treat in your hand as you approach within a foot of the dog.

TRAINING TIP

Dogs will do anything for your attention. If you reward the dog when he is attentive and calm, you will develop a well-mannered dog. If, on the other hand, you greet your dog excitedly and encourage him to wrestle with you, the dog will greet you the same way and you will have an hyperactive dog on your hands.

THE GOLDEN RULE

The golden rule of dog training is simple. For each 'question' (command), there is only one correct answer (reaction). One command = one reaction. Keep practising the command until the dog reacts correctly without hesitating. Be repetitive but not monotonous. Dogs get bored just as people do!

Do not go directly to him, but stop about a foot short of him and hold out the treat as you ask 'School?' He will see you approaching with a treat in your hand and most likely begin walking toward you. As you meet, give him the treat and praise again.

The third time, ask the question, have a treat in your hand and walk only a short distance toward the dog so that he must walk almost all the way to you. As he reaches you, give him

the treat and praise again.

By this time, the dog will probably be getting the idea that if he pays attention to you, especially when you ask that question, it will pay off in treats and enjoyable activities for him. In other words, he learns that 'school' means doing great things with you that are fun and that result in positive attention for him.

COMMAND STANCE

Stand up straight and authoritatively when giving your dog commands. Do not issue commands when lying on the floor or lying on your back on the sofa. If you are on your hands and knees when you give a command, your dog will think you are positioning yourself to play.

Remember that the dog does not understand your verbal language; he only recognises sounds. Your question translates to a series of sounds for him, and those sounds become the signal to go to you and pay attention. The dog learns that if he does this, he will get to interact with you plus receive treats and praise.

The pup will learn to sit without even knowing it! Initiate the exercise by holding up a treat, and the pup will assume the sit position as he looks up and reaches for it.

Most of all, be positive when approaching the training of your King Charles Spaniel. This is an intelligent and sensitive breed that responds reliably to praise and kindness.

THE BASIC COMMANDS

TEACHING THE SIT EXERCISE

Now that you have the dog's attention, attach his lead and hold it in your left hand, and hold a food treat in your right hand. Place your food hand at the dog's nose and let him lick the treat but not take it from you. Say 'Sit' and slowly raise your food hand from in front of the dog's nose up over his head so that he is looking at the ceiling. As he bends his head upward, he will have to bend his knees to maintain his balance. As he bends his knees, he will assume a sit position. At that point, release the food treat and praise lavishly with comments such as 'Good dog! Good sit!,' etc. Remember to always praise enthusiastically, because dogs relish verbal praise from their owners and feel so proud of themselves whenever they accomplish a behaviour.

You will not use food forever in getting the dog to obey your commands. Food is only used to teach new behaviours and, once the dog knows what you want when you give a specific command, you will wean him off the food treats but still maintain the verbal praise. After all, you will always have your voice with you, and there will be many times when you have no food rewards but expect the dog to obey.

TEACHING THE DOWN EXERCISE

Teaching the the down exercise is easy when you understand how the dog perceives the down position, and it is very difficult

> **TRAINING RULES**
> If you want to be successful in training your dog, you have four rules to obey yourself:
> 1. Develop an understanding of how a dog thinks.
> 2. Do not blame the dog for lack of communication.
> 3. Define your dog's personality and act accordingly.
> 4. Have patience and be consistent.

when you do not. Dogs perceive the down position as a submissive one; therefore, teaching the down exercise by using a forceful method can sometimes make the dog develop such a fear of the down that he either runs away when you say 'Down' or he attempts to snap at the person who tries to force him down.

Have the dog sit close alongside your left leg, facing in the same direction as you are. Hold the lead in your left hand and a food treat in your right. Now place your left hand lightly on the top of the dog's shoulders where they meet above the spinal cord. Do not push down on the dog's shoulders; simply rest your left hand there so you can guide the dog to lie down close to your left leg rather than to swing away from your side when he drops.

Now place the food hand at the dog's nose, say 'Down' very softly (almost a whisper) and slowly lower the food hand to the dog's front feet. When the food hand reaches the floor, begin moving it forward along the floor in front of the dog. Keep talking softly to the dog, saying things like, 'Do you want this treat? You can do this, good dog.' Your reassuring tone of voice will help calm the dog as he tries to follow the food hand in order to get the treat.

When the dog's elbows touch the floor, release the food and

Teaching the dog to sit is a very basic exercise and a necessity for a politely behaved dog.

praise softly. Try to get the dog to maintain that down position for several seconds before you let him sit up again. The goal here is to get the dog to settle down and not feel threatened in the down position.

TEACHING THE STAY EXERCISE

It is easy to teach the dog to stay in either a sit or a down position. Again, we use food and praise during the teaching process as we help the dog to understand

DOUBLE JEOPARDY
A dog in jeopardy never lies down. He stays alert on his feet because instinct tells him that he may have to run away or fight for his survival. Therefore, if a dog feels threatened or anxious, he will not lie down. Consequently, it is important to keep the dog calm and relaxed as he learns the down exercise.

exactly what it is that we are expecting him to do.

To teach the sit/stay, start with the dog sitting on your left side as before and hold the lead in your left hand. Have a food treat in your right hand and place your food hand at the dog's nose. Say 'Stay' and step out on your right foot to stand directly in front of the dog, toe to toe, as he licks and nibbles the treat. Be sure to keep his head facing upward to maintain the sit position. Count to five and then swing around to stand next to the dog again with him on your left. As soon as you get back to the original position, release the food and praise lavishly.

To teach the down/stay, do the down as previously described. As soon as the dog lies down, say 'Stay' and step out on your right foot just as you did in the sit/stay. Count to five and then return to stand beside the dog with him on your left side. Release the treat and praise as always.

Within a week to ten days, you can begin to add a bit of distance between you and your dog when you leave him. When you do, use your left hand open with the palm facing the dog as a stay signal, much the same as the hand signal a constable uses to stop traffic at a junction. Hold the food treat in your right hand as before, but this time the food will not be touching the dog's nose. He will watch the food hand and quickly learn that he is going to get that treat as soon as you return to his side.

When you can stand 1 metre away from your dog for 30 seconds, you can then begin building time and distance in both stays. Eventually, the dog can be expected to remain in the stay position for prolonged periods of time until you return to him or call him to you. Always praise lavishly when he stays.

TEACHING THE COME EXERCISE
If you make teaching 'come' an exciting experience, you should never have a 'student' that does not love the game or that fails to

ATTENTION!
Your dog is actually training you at the same time you are training him. Dogs do things to get attention. They usually repeat whatever succeeds in getting your attention.

Teaching the down exercise may require a little extra coaxing and reassurance—and a food reward always helps!

The intelligent and alert King Charles Spaniel makes a bright and attentive student.

Everyone takes turns calling the dog, and each person should celebrate the dog's finding him with a treat and lots of happy praise. When a person calls the dog, he is actually inviting the dog to find him and to get a treat as a reward for 'winning.'

A few turns of the 'Where are you?' game and the dog will understand that everyone is playing the game and that each person has a big celebration awaiting the dog's success at locating him or her. Once the dog learns to love the game, simply calling out 'Where are you?' will bring him running from wherever he is when he hears that all-important question.

The come command is recognised as one of the most important things to teach a dog, but there are trainers who work

come when called. The secret, it seems, is never to teach the word 'come.'

At times when an owner most wants his dog to come when called, the owner is likely to be upset or anxious and he allows these feelings to come through in the tone of his voice when he calls his dog. Hearing that desperation in his owner's voice, the dog fears the results of going to him and therefore either disobeys outright or runs in the opposite direction. The secret, therefore, is to teach the dog a game and, when you want him to come to you, simply play the game. It is practically a no-fail solution!

To begin, have several members of your family take a few food treats and each go into a different room in the house.

CONSISTENCY PAYS OFF

Dogs need consistency in their feeding times, exercise and toilet breaks, and in the verbal commands you use. If you use 'Stay' on Monday and 'Stay here, please' on Tuesday, you will confuse your dog. Don't demand perfect behaviour during training classes and then let him have the run of the house the rest of the day. Above all, lavish praise on your pet consistently every time he does something right. The more he feels he is pleasing you, the more willing he will be to learn.

FEAR AGGRESSION

Pups who are subjected to physical abuse during training commonly end up with behavioural problems as adults. One common result of abuse is fear aggression, in which a dog will lash out, bare his teeth, snarl and finally bite someone by whom he feels threatened. For example, your daughter may be playing with the dog one afternoon. As they play hide-and-seek, she backs the dog into a corner and, as she attempts to tease him playfully, he bites her hand. Examine the cause of this behaviour. Did your daughter ever hit the dog? Did someone who resembles your daughter hit or scream at the dog?

Fortunately, fear aggression is relatively easy to correct. Have your daughter engage in only positive activities with the dog, such as feeding, petting and walking. She should not give any corrections or negative feedback. If the dog still growls or cowers away from her, allow someone else to accompany them. After approximately one week, the dog should feel that he can rely on her for many positive things, and he will also be prevented from reacting fearfully towards anyone who might resemble her.

with thousands of dogs and never teach the actual word 'come.' Yet these dogs will race to respond to a person who uses the dog's name followed by 'Where are you?' For example, a woman has a 12-year-old companion dog who went blind, but who never fails to locate her owner when asked, 'Where are you?'

Children, in particular, love to play this game with their dogs. Children can hide in smaller places like a shower or bath, behind a bed or under a table. The dog needs to work a little bit harder to find these hiding places, but, when he does, he loves to celebrate with a treat and a tussle with a favourite youngster.

'COME' . . . BACK

Never call your dog to come to you for a correction or scold him when he reaches you. That is the quickest way to turn a 'Come' command into 'Go away fast!' Dogs think only in the present tense, and your dog will connect the scolding with coming to you, not with the misbehaviour of a few moments earlier.

TEACHING THE HEEL EXERCISE

Heeling means that the dog walks beside the owner without pulling. It takes time and patience on the owner's part to succeed at teaching the dog that he (the owner) will not proceed unless the dog is walking calmly beside him. Neither pulling out ahead on the lead nor lagging behind is acceptable.

Begin by holding the lead in your left hand as the dog sits beside your left leg. Move the loop end of the lead to your right hand, but keep your left hand short on the lead so that it keeps the dog in close next to you.

Say 'Heel' and step forward on your left foot. Keep the dog close to you and take three steps.

'WHERE ARE YOU?'

When calling the dog, do not say 'Come.' Say things like, 'Rover, where are you? See if you can find me! I have a biscuit for you!' Keep up a constant line of chatter with coaxing sounds and frequent questions such as, 'Where are you?' The dog will learn to follow the sound of your voice to locate you and receive his reward.

SAFETY FIRST

While it may seem that the most important things to your dog are eating, sleeping and chewing the upholstery on your furniture, his first concern is actually safety. The domesticated dogs we keep as companions have the same pack instinct as their ancestors who ran free thousands of years ago. Because of this pack instinct, your dog wants to know that he and his pack are not in danger of being harmed, and that his pack has a strong, capable leader. You must establish yourself as the leader early on in your relationship. That way, your dog will trust that you will take care of him and the pack, and he will accept your commands without question.

Stop and have the dog sit next to you in what we now call the 'heel position.' Praise verbally, but do not touch the dog. Hesitate a moment and begin again with 'Heel,' taking three steps and stopping, at which point the dog is told to sit again.

Your goal here is to have the dog walk those three steps without pulling on the lead. Once he will walk calmly beside you for three steps without pulling, increase the number of steps you take to five. When he will walk politely beside you while you take five steps, you can increase the length of your walk to ten steps.

HEELING WELL

Teach your dog to HEEL in an enclosed area. Once you think the dog will obey reliably and you want to attempt advanced obedience exercises such as off-lead heeling, test him in a fenced-in area so he cannot run away.

Keep increasing the length of your stroll until the dog will walk quietly beside you without pulling as long as you want him

THE STUDENT'S STRESS TEST

During training sessions, you must be able to recognise signs of stress in your dog such as:

- tucking his tail between his legs
- lowering his head
- shivering or trembling
- standing completely still or running away
- panting and/or salivating
- avoiding eye contact
- flattening his ears back
- urinating submissively
- rolling over and lifting a leg
- grinning or baring teeth
- aggression when restrained

If your four-legged student displays these signs, he may just be nervous or intimidated. The training session may have been too lengthy, with not enough praise and affirmation. Stop for the day and try again tomorrow.

to heel. When you stop heeling, indicate to the dog that the exercise is over by verbally praising as you pet him and say 'OK, good dog.' The 'OK' is used as a release word, meaning that the exercise is finished and the dog is free to relax.

If you are dealing with a dog who insists on pulling you around, simply 'put on your

Your King Charles must be taught to behave on lead so that he will act appropriately when the two of you are out and about.

Each time the dog looks up at you or slows down to give a slack lead between the two of you, quietly praise him and say, 'Good heel. Good dog.' Eventually, the dog will begin to respond and within a few days he will be walking politely beside you without pulling on the lead. At first, the training sessions should be kept short and they should always be very positive; soon the dog will be able to walk nicely with you for increasingly longer distances. Remember also to give the dog free

TUG OF WALK?

If you begin teaching the heel by taking long walks and letting the dog pull you along, he misinterprets this action as an acceptable form of taking a walk. When you pull back on the lead to counteract his pulling, he reads that tug as a signal to pull even harder!

brakes' and stand your ground until the dog realises that the two of you are not going anywhere until he is beside you and moving at your pace, not his. It may take some time just standing there to convince the dog that you are the leader and that you will be the one to decide on the direction and speed of your travel.

HOW TO WEAN THE 'TREAT HOG'

If you have trained your dog by rewarding him with a treat each time he performs a command, he may soon decide that, without the treat, he won't sit, stay or come. The best way to fix this problem is to start asking your dog to do certain commands twice before being rewarded. Slowly increase the number of commands given and then vary the number: three sits and a treat one day, five sits for a biscuit the next day, etc. Your dog will soon realise that there is no set number of sits before he gets his reward, and he'll likely do it the first time you ask in the hope of being rewarded sooner rather than later.

'NO' MEANS 'NO!'

Dogs do not understand our language. They can be trained to react to a certain sound, at a certain volume. If you say 'No, Oliver' in a very soft pleasant voice, it will not have the same meaning as 'No, Oliver!!' when you raise your voice. You should never use the dog's name during a reprimand, just the command NO!!

Since dogs don't understand words, comics often use dogs trained with opposite meanings. Thus, when the comic commands his dog to SIT, the dog will stand up, and vice versa.

Once your King Charles is heel-trained, your daily walks will be enjoyable outings for both of you.

time and the opportunity to run and play when you have finished heel practice.

WEANING OFF FOOD IN TRAINING

Food is used in training new behaviours. Once the dog understands what behaviour goes with a specific command, it is time to start weaning him off the food treats. At first, give a treat after each exercise. Then, start to give a treat only after every other

TRAINING TIP

If you are walking your dog and he suddenly stops and looks straight into your eyes, ignore him. Pull the leash and lead him into the direction you want to walk.

exercise. Mix up the times when you offer a food reward and the times when you only offer praise so that the dog will never know when he is going to receive both food and praise and when he is going to receive only praise. This is called a variable ratio reward system. It proves successful because there is always the chance that the owner will produce a treat, so the dog never stops trying for that reward. No matter what, *always* give verbal praise.

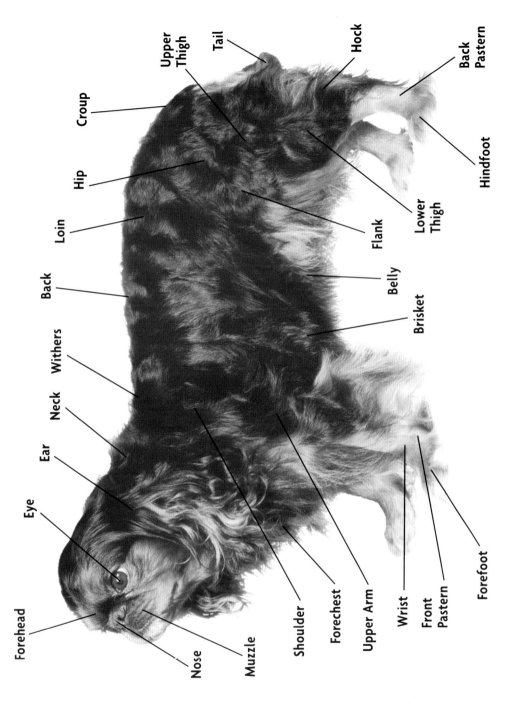

PHYSICAL STRUCTURE OF THE KING CHARLES SPANIEL

Dogs suffer from many of the same physical illnesses as people. Since people usually know more about human diseases than canine maladies, many of the terms used in this chapter will be familiar but not necessarily those used by veterinary surgeons. We will use the term *x-ray*, instead of the more acceptable term *radiograph*. We will also use the familiar term *symptoms* even though dogs don't have symptoms, which are verbal descriptions of the patient's feelings; dogs have *clinical signs*. Since dogs can't speak, we have to look for clinical signs...but we still use the term *symptoms* in this book.

As a general rule, medicine is *practised*. That term is not arbitrary. Medicine is a constantly changing art as we learn more and more about genetics, electronic aids (like CAT scans and MRIs) and daily laboratory advances. There are many dog maladies, like canine hip dysplasia, which are not universally treated in the same manner. Some veterinary surgeons opt for surgery more often than others do.

SELECTING A VETERINARY SURGEON

Your selection of a veterinary surgeon should be based upon his reputation for his skills with small animals, especially dogs, and particularly toy dogs if possible. You want a vet who is close by because you might have emergencies or need to make multiple visits for treatments. You want a vet who has services that you might require such as tattooing and grooming, as well as sophisticated pet supplies and a good reputation for ability and responsiveness. There is nothing more frustrating than having to wait a day or more to get a response from your veterinary surgeon.

All veterinary surgeons are licenced and their diplomas and/or certificates should be displayed in their waiting rooms. There are, however, many veteri-

PROPER DIET

Feeding your dog properly is very important. An incorrect diet could affect the dog's health, behaviour and nervous system, possibly making a normal dog into an aggressive one. Its most visible effects are to the skin and coat, but internal organs are similary affected.

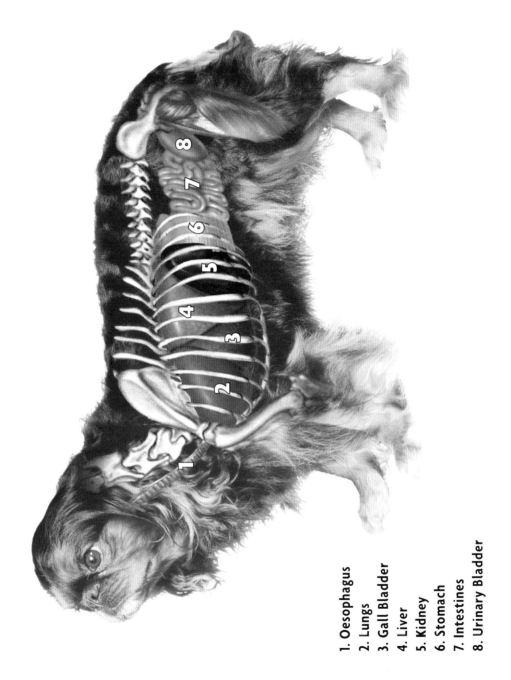

1. Oesophagus
2. Lungs
3. Gall Bladder
4. Liver
5. Kidney
6. Stomach
7. Intestines
8. Urinary Bladder

INTERNAL ORGANS OF THE KING CHARLES SPANIEL

nary specialities that usually require further studies and internships. There are specialists in heart problems (veterinary cardiologists), skin problems (veterinary dermatologists), teeth and gum problems (veterinary dentists), eye problems (veterinary ophthalmologists) and x-rays (veterinary radiologists), as well as vets who have specialities in bones, muscles or other organs. Most veterinary surgeons do routine surgery such as neutering, stitching up wounds and docking tails for those breeds in which such is required for show purposes.

When the problem affecting your dog is serious, it is not unusual or impudent to get another medical opinion, although in Britain you are obliged to advise the vets concerned about this. You might also want to compare costs among several veterinary surgeons. Sophisticated health care and veterinary services can be very costly. It is not infrequent that treatment options are chosen based upon financial considerations.

PREVENTATIVE MEDICINE

It is much easier, less costly and more effective to practise preventative medicine than to fight bouts of illness and disease. Properly bred puppies come from parents who were selected based upon their genetic disease profiles. Their mothers should have been

Breakdown of Veterinary Income by Category

2%	Dentistry
4%	Radiology
12%	Surgery
15%	Vaccinations
19%	Laboratory
23%	Examinations
25%	Medicines

A typical American vet's income, categorised according to services performed. This survey dealt with small-animal (pets) practices.

vaccinated, free of all internal and external parasites and properly nourished. The dam can pass on disease resistance to her puppies, which can last for eight to ten weeks, but she can also pass on parasites and many infections. For these reasons, a visit to the veterinary surgeon who cared for the dam is recommended.

WEANING TO FIVE MONTHS OLD

Puppies should be weaned by the time they are about two months old. A puppy that remains for at least eight weeks with its mother and littermates usually adapts better to other dogs and people later in life. Some new owners have their puppies examined by veterinary surgeons immediately, which is a good idea. Vaccination programmes usually begin when the puppy is very young.

The puppy will have its teeth

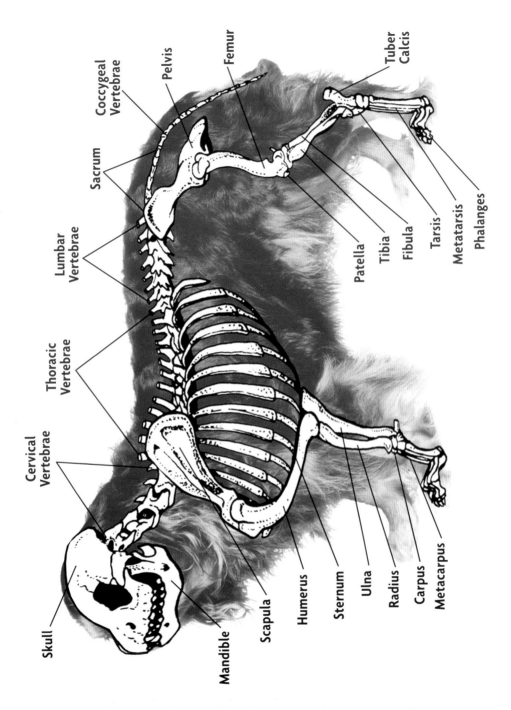

SKELETAL STRUCTURE OF THE KING CHARLES SPANIEL

examined, and have its skeletal conformation and general health checked prior to certification by the veterinary surgeon. Puppies in certain breeds may have problems with their kneecaps, cataracts and other eye problems, heart murmurs or undescended testicles. They may also have personality problems, and your veterinary surgeon might have training in temperament evaluation.

VACCINATIONS

Most vaccinations are given by injection and should only be done by a veterinary surgeon. Both he and you should keep records of the date of the injection, the identification of the vaccine and the amount given. Some vets give a first vaccination at eight weeks, but most dog breeders prefer the course not to commence until about ten weeks to avoid negating any antibodies passed on by the dam. The vaccination timetable is usually based on a 15-day cycle. You must take your vet's advice regarding when to vaccinate, as this may differ according to the vaccine used. Most vaccinations immunize your puppy against viruses.

The usual vaccines contain immunizing doses of several different viruses such as

HEALTH AND VACCINATION TIMETABLE

AGE IN WEEKS:	6TH	8TH	10TH	12TH	14TH	16TH	20-24TH	52ND
Worm Control	✔	✔	✔	✔	✔	✔	✔	
Neutering								✔
Heartworm		✔		✔		✔	✔	
Parvovirus	✔		✔		✔		✔	✔
Distemper		✔		✔		✔		✔
Hepatitis		✔		✔		✔		✔
Leptospirosis								✔
Parainfluenza	✔		✔		✔			✔
Dental Examination		✔					✔	✔
Complete Physical		✔					✔	✔
Coronavirus				✔			✔	✔
Kennel Cough	✔							
Hip Dysplasia								✔
Rabies							✔	

Vaccinations are not instantly effective. It takes about two weeks for the dog's immune system to develop antibodies. Most vaccinations require annual booster shots. Your veterinary surgeon should guide you in this regard.

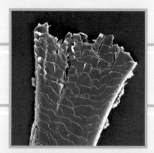
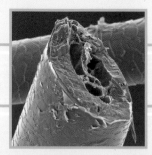

Normal hairs of a dog enlarged 200 times original size. The cuticle (outer covering) is clean and healthy. Unlike human hair that grows from the base, a dog's hair also grows from the end. Damaged hairs and split ends, illustrated above.

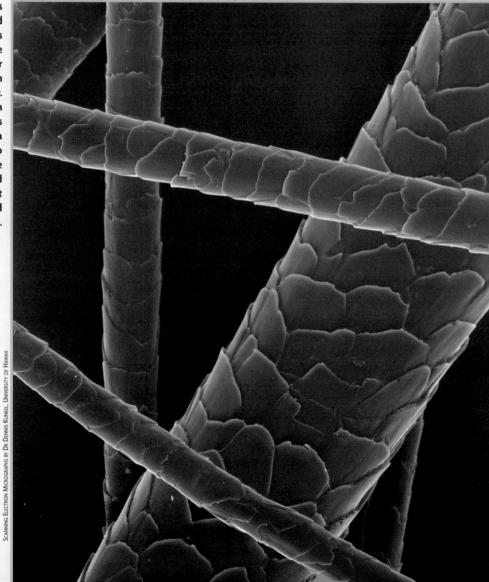

SCANNING ELECTRON MICROGRAPHS BY DR. DENNIS KUNKEL, UNIVERSITY OF HAWAII

DISEASE REFERENCE CHART

	What is it?	What causes it?	Symptoms
Leptospirosis	Severe disease that affects the internal organs; can be spread to people.	A bacterium, which is often carried by rodents, that enters through mucous membranes and spreads quickly throughout the body.	Range from fever, vomiting and loss of appetite in less severe cases to shock, irreversible kidney damage and possibly death in most severe cases.
Rabies	Potentially deadly virus that infects warm-blooded mammals. Not seen in United Kingdom.	Bite from a carrier of the virus, mainly wild animals.	1st stage: dog exhibits change in behaviour, fear. 2nd stage: dog's behaviour becomes more aggressive. 3rd stage: loss of coordination, trouble with bodily functions.
Parvovirus	Highly contagious virus, potentially deadly.	Ingestion of the virus, which is usually spread through the faeces of infected dogs.	Most common: severe diarrhoea. Also vomiting, fatigue, lack of appetite.
Kennel cough	Contagious respiratory infection.	Combination of types of bacteria and virus. Most common: *Bordetella bronchiseptica* bacteria and parainfluenza virus.	Chronic cough.
Distemper	Disease primarily affecting respiratory and nervous system.	Virus that is related to the human measles virus.	Mild symptoms such as fever, lack of appetite and mucous secretion progress to evidence of brain damage, 'hard pad.'
Hepatitis	Virus primarily affecting the liver.	Canine adenovirus type I (CAV-1). Enters system when dog breathes in particles.	Lesser symptoms include listlessness, diarrhoea, vomiting. More severe symptoms include 'blue-eye' (clumps of virus in eye).
Coronavirus	Virus resulting in digestive problems.	Virus is spread through infected dog's faeces.	Stomach upset evidenced by lack of appetite, vomiting, diarrhoea.

distemper, parvovirus, parainfluenza and hepatitis, although some veterinary surgeons recommend separate vaccines for each disease. There are other vaccines available when the puppy is at risk. You should rely upon professional advice. This is especially true for the booster-shot programme. Most vaccination programmes require a booster when the puppy is a year old and once a year thereafter. In some cases, circumstances may require more or less frequent immunizations. Kennel cough, more formally known as tracheobronchitis, is treated with a vaccine that is sprayed into the dog's nostrils. Kennel cough is usually included in routine vaccination, but this is often not so effective as for other major diseases.

FIVE TO TWELVE MONTHS OF AGE
Unless you intend to breed or show your dog, neutering the puppy at six months of age is recommended. Discuss this with your veterinary surgeon. Neutering/spaying has proven to be extremely beneficial to male and female puppies, respectively. Besides eliminating the possibility of pregnancy, it inhibits (but does not prevent) breast cancer in

bitches and prostate cancer in male dogs. Under no circumstances should a bitch be spayed prior to her first season.

Your veterinary surgeon should provide your puppy with a thorough dental evaluation at six months of age, ascertaining whether all the permanent teeth have erupted properly. An home dental-care regimen should be initiated at six months, including brushing weekly and providing good dental devices (such as nylon bones). Regular dental care promotes healthy teeth, fresh breath and a longer life.

ONE TO SEVEN YEARS

Once a year, your grown dog should visit the vet for an examination and vaccination boosters, if needed. Some vets recommend blood tests, a thyroid level check and a dental evaluation to accompany these annual visits. A thorough clinical evaluation by the vet can provide critical background information for your dog. Blood tests are often performed at one year of age, and dental examinations around the third or fourth birthday. In the long run, quality preventative care for your pet can save money, teeth and lives.

SKIN PROBLEMS

Veterinary surgeons are consulted by dog owners for skin problems more than for any other group of diseases or maladies. Dogs' skin is almost as sensitive as human skin, and both suffer from almost the same ailments (though the occurrence of acne in dogs is rare!). For this reason, veterinary dermatology has developed into a speciality practised by many veterinary surgeons.

Since many skin problems have visual symptoms that are almost identical, it requires the skill of an experienced veterinary dermatologist to identify and cure many of the more severe skin disorders. Pet shops sell many treatments for skin problems, but most of the treatments are directed at the symptoms and not the underlying problem(s). If your dog is suffering from a skin disorder, you should seek professional assistance as quickly as possible. As with all diseases, the earlier a problem is identified and treated, the better the chances are that the cure will be successful.

HEREDITARY SKIN DISORDERS

Veterinary dermatologists are currently researching a number of skin disorders that are believed to have an hereditary basis. These inherited diseases are transmitted by both parents, who appear (phenotypically) normal but have a recessive gene for the disease, meaning that they carry, but are not affected by, the disease. These diseases pose serious problems to

VACCINE ALLERGIES
Vaccines do not work all the time. Sometimes dogs are allergic to them and many times the antibodies, which are supposed to be stimulated by the vaccine, just are not produced. You should keep your dog in the veterinary clinic for an hour after he is vaccinated to be sure there are no allergic reactions.

breeders because in some instances there are no methods of identifying carriers. Often the secondary diseases associated with these skin conditions are even more debilitating than the skin disorders themselves, including cancers and respiratory problems.

Among the hereditary skin disorders, for which the mode of inheritance is known, are acro-dermatitis, cutaneous asthenia (Ehlers-Danlos syndrome), sebaceous adenitis, cyclic hematopoiesis, dermatomyositis, IgA deficiency, colour dilution alopaecia and nodular dermatofi-brosis. Some of these disorders are limited to one or two breeds, while others affect a large number of breeds. All inherited diseases must be diagnosed and treated by a veterinary specialist.

PARASITE BITES
Many of us are allergic to insect bites. The bites itch, erupt and may even become infected. Dogs have the same reaction to fleas, ticks and/or mites. When an insect lands on you, you have the chance to whisk it away with your hand. Unfortunately, when your dog is bitten by a flea, tick or mite, he can only scratch it away or bite it. By the time the dog has been bitten, the parasite has done some of its damage. It may also have laid eggs, which will cause further problems in the near future. The itching from parasite bites is probably due to the saliva injected into the site when the parasite sucks the dog's blood.

AUTO-IMMUNE SKIN CONDITIONS
An auto-immune skin condition is commonly referred to as a condition in which a person (or dog) is 'allergic' to him- or herself, while an allergy is usually an inflammatory reaction to an outside stimulus. Auto-immune diseases cause serious damage to the tissues that are involved.

The best known auto-immune disease is lupus, which affects people as well as dogs. The symptoms are variable and may affect the kidneys, bones, blood chemistry and skin. It can be fatal to both dogs and humans, though it is not thought to be transmis-sible. It is usually successfully treated with cortisone, pred-nisone or a similar corticosteroid, but extensive use of these drugs can have harmful side effects.

AIRBORNE ALLERGIES

Just as humans suffer from hay fever, rose fever and other fevers during the pollinating season, many dogs suffer from the same allergies. When the pollen count is high, your dog might suffer, but don't expect him to sneeze and have a runny nose as a human would. Dogs react to pollen allergies in the same way they react to fleas—they scratch and bite themselves. Dogs, like humans, can be tested for allergens. Discuss the testing with your veterinary dermatologist.

FOOD PROBLEMS

FOOD ALLERGIES

Dogs are allergic to many foods that are best-sellers and highly recommended by breeders and veterinary surgeons. Changing the brand of food that you buy may not eliminate the problem if the element to which the dog is allergic is contained in the new brand.

Recognising a food allergy is difficult. Humans vomit or have rashes when they eat a food to which they are allergic. Dogs neither vomit nor (usually) develop rashes. They react in the same manner as they would to an airborne or flea allergy; they itch, scratch and bite, thus making the diagnosis extremely difficult. While pollen allergies and parasite bites are usually seasonal, food allergies are year-round problems.

FOOD INTOLERANCE

Food intolerance is the inability of the dog to completely digest certain foods. Puppies that may

---

BE CAREFUL WHERE YOU WALK YOUR DOG

Dogs who have been exposed to lawns sprayed with herbicides have double and triple the rate of malignant lymphoma. Town dogs are especially at risk, as they are exposed to tailored lawns and gardens. Dogs perspire and absorb through their footpads. Be careful where your dog walks and always avoid any area that appears yellowed from chemical overspray. These chemicals are not good for you, either!

have done very well on their mother's milk may not do well on cow's milk. The results of food intolerance may be evident in loose bowels, passing gas and stomach pains. These are the only obvious symptoms of food intolerance, which makes diagnosis difficult.

TREATING FOOD PROBLEMS

It is possible to handle food allergies and food intolerance yourself. Start by putting your dog on a diet that he has never had. Obviously, if the dog has never eaten this new food, he can't have been allergic or intolerant of it. Start with a single ingredient that is not in the dog's diet at the present time. Ingredients like chopped beef or fish are common in dogs' diets, so try something more exotic like rabbit, pheasant or another protein source. Keep the dog on this diet (with no additives) for a month. If the symptoms of food allergy or intolerance disappear, it is quite likely that your dog has a food allergy.

Don't think that the single ingredient cured the problem. You still must find a suitable diet and ascertain which ingredient in the old diet was objectionable. This is most easily done by adding ingredients to the new diet one at a time. Let the dog stay on the modified diet for a month before you add another ingredient.

DENTAL DEMANDS

You are your dog's caretaker and his dentist. Vets warn that plaque and tartar buildup on the teeth will damage the gums and allow bacteria to enter the dog's bloodstream, causing serious damage to the animal's vital organs. Studies show that over 50 percent of dogs have some form of gum disease before age three. Daily or weekly tooth cleaning (with a brush or soft gauze pad wipes and a canine toothpaste) can add years to your dog's life.

Eventually, you will determine the ingredient that caused the adverse reaction.

An alternative method is to carefully study the ingredients in the diet to which your dog is allergic or intolerant. Identify the main ingredient in this diet and eliminate the main ingredient by buying a different food that does not have that ingredient. Keep experimenting until the symptoms disappear after one month on the new diet.

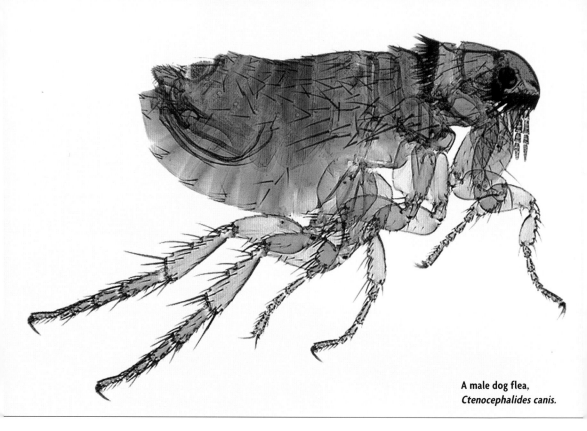

A male dog flea,
Ctenocephalides canis.

EXTERNAL PARASITES

FLEAS

Of all the problems to which dogs are prone, none is more well known and frustrating than fleas. Flea infestation is relatively simple to cure but difficult to prevent. Parasites that are harboured inside the body are a bit more difficult to eradicate but they are easier to control.

To control flea infestation, you have to understand the flea's life cycle. Fleas are often thought of as a summertime problem, but centrally heated homes have changed the patterns and fleas can be found at any time of the year.

The most effective method of flea control is a two-stage approach: one stage to kill the adult fleas, and the other to control the development of pre-adult fleas. Unfortunately, no single active ingredient is effective against all stages of the life cycle.

LIFE CYCLE STAGES

During its life, a flea will pass through four life stages: egg, larva, pupa and adult. The adult stage is the most visible and irritating stage of the flea life cycle, and this is why the majority of flea-control products concentrate on this stage. The fact is that adult fleas account for only 1% of the total flea population, and the other 99% exist in pre-adult stages, i.e. eggs, larvae and pupae. The pre-adult stages are barely visible to the naked eye.

The Life Cycle of the Flea

Eggs are laid on the dog, usually in quantities of about 20 or 30, several times a day. The adult female flea must have a blood meal before each egg-laying session. When first laid, the eggs will cling to the dog's hair, as the eggs are still moist. However, they will quickly dry out and fall from the dog, especially if the dog moves around or scratches. Many eggs will fall off in the dog's favourite area or an area in which he spends a lot of time, such as his bed.

Once the eggs fall from the dog onto the carpet or furniture, they will hatch into larvae. This takes from one to ten days. Larvae are not particularly mobile and will usually travel only a few

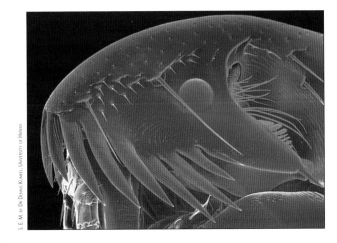

S. E. M. by Dr Dennis Kunkel, University of Hawaii

inches from where they hatch. However, they do have a tendency to move away from light and heavy traffic—under furniture and behind doors are common places to find high quantities of flea larvae.

The flea larvae feed on dead organic matter, including adult flea faeces, until they are ready to change into adult fleas. Fleas will usually remain as larvae for around seven days. After this period, the larvae will pupate into protective pupae. While inside the pupae, the larvae will undergo metamorphosis and change into adult fleas. This can take as little time as a few days, but the adult fleas can remain inside the pupae waiting to hatch for up to two years. The pupae are signalled to hatch by certain stimuli, such as physical pressure—the pupae's being stepped on, heat from an animal's lying on the pupae or

Magnified head of a dog flea, *Ctenocephalides canis*, colorized for effect.

FLEA KILLERS

Flea-killers are poisonous. You should not spray these toxic chemicals on areas of a dog's body that he licks, including his genitals and his face. Flea killers taken internally are a better answer, but check with your vet in case internal therapy is not advised for your dog.

The dog flea is the most common parasite found on pet dogs.

S. E. M. BY DR DENNIS KUNKEL, UNIVERSITY OF HAWAII

increased carbon-dioxide levels and vibrations—indicating that a suitable host is available.

Once hatched, the adult flea must feed within a few days. Once the adult flea finds an host, it will not leave voluntarily. It only becomes dislodged by grooming or the host animal's scratching. The adult flea will remain on the host for the duration of its life unless forcibly removed.

Dwight R Kuhn's magnificent action photo, showing a flea jumping from a dog's back.

PHOTO BY DWIGHT R KUHN

TREATING THE ENVIRONMENT AND THE DOG

Treating fleas should be a two-pronged attack. First, the environment needs to be treated; this includes carpets and furniture, especially the dog's bedding and areas underneath furniture. The environment should be treated with an household spray containing an Insect Growth Regulator (IGR) and an insecticide to kill the adult fleas. Most IGRs are effective against eggs and larvae; they actually mimic the fleas' own hormones and stop the eggs and larvae from developing into adult fleas. There are currently no treatments available to attack the pupa stage of the life cycle, so the adult insecticide is used to kill the newly hatched adult fleas before they find an host. Most IGRs are active for many months, while adult insecticides are only active for a few days.

When treating with an household spray, it is a good idea to vacuum before applying the product. This stimulates as many pupae as possible to hatch into adult fleas. The vacuum cleaner should also be treated with an insecticide to prevent the eggs and larvae that have been hoovered into the vacuum bag from hatching.

The second stage of treatment is to apply an adult insecticide to

EN GARDE:
CATCHING FLEAS OFF GUARD!

Consider the following ways to arm yourself against fleas:

- Add a small amount of pennyroyal or eucalyptus oil to your dog's bath. These natural remedies repel fleas.
- Supplement your dog's food with fresh garlic (minced or grated) and an hearty amount of brewer's yeast, both of which ward off fleas.
- Use a flea comb on your dog daily. Submerge fleas in a cup of bleach to kill them quickly.
- Confine the dog to only a few rooms to limit the spread of fleas in the home.
- Vacuum daily...and get all of the crevices! Dispose of the bag every few days until the problem is under control.
- Wash your dog's bedding daily. Cover cushions where your dog sleeps with towels, and wash the towels often.

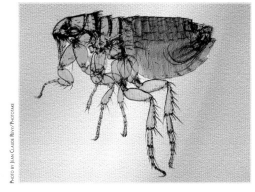

A LOOK AT FLEAS

Fleas have been around for millions of years and have adapted to changing host animals. They are able to go through a complete life cycle in less than one month or they can extend their lives to almost two years by remaining as pupae or cocoons. They do not need blood or any other food for up to 20 months.

They have been measured as being able to jump 300,000 times and can jump 150 times their length in any direction, including straight up. Those are just a few of the reasons why they are so successful in infesting a dog!

THE LIFE CYCLE OF THE FLEA

Eggs

Larvae

Pupa

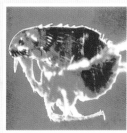

Adult

A scanning electron micrograph of a dog or cat flea, *Ctenocephalides*, magnified more than 100x. This image has been colorized for effect.

the dog. Traditionally, this would be in the form of a collar or a spray, but more recent innovations include digestible insecticides that poison the fleas when they ingest the dog's blood. Alternatively, there are drops that, when placed on the back of the dog's neck, spread throughout the hair and skin to kill adult fleas.

INSECT GROWTH REGULATOR (IGR)

Two types of products should be used when treating fleas—a product to treat the pet and a product to treat the home. Adult fleas represent less than 1% of the flea population. The pre-adult fleas (eggs, larvae and pupae) represent more than 99% of the flea population and are found in the environment; it is in the case of pre-adult fleas that products containing an Insect Growth Regulator (IGR) should be used in the home.

IGRs are a new class of compounds used to prevent the development of insects. They do not kill the insect outright, but instead use the insect's biology against it to stop it from completing its growth. Products that contain methoprene are the world's first and leading IGRs. Used to control fleas and other insects, this type of IGR will stop flea larvae from developing and protect the house for up to seven months.

DID YOU KNOW?
Never mix flea control products without first consulting your vet. Some products can become toxic when combined with others and can cause fatal consequences.

TICKS AND MITES

Though not as common as fleas, ticks and mites are found all over the tropical and temperate world. They don't bite, like fleas; they harpoon. They dig their sharp proboscis (nose) into the dog's skin and drink the blood. Their only food and drink is dog's blood. Dogs can get Lyme disease, Rocky Mountain spotted fever (normally found in the US only), paralysis and many other diseases from ticks and mites. They may live where fleas are found and they like to hide in cracks or seams in walls. They are controlled the same way fleas are controlled.

The dog tick, *Dermacentor variabilis*, may well be the most common dog tick in many geographical areas, especially those areas where the climate is hot and humid. Most dog ticks

A brown dog tick, *Rhipicephalus sanguineus*, is an uncommon but annoying tick found on dogs.
PHOTO BY CAROLINA BIOLOGICAL SUPPLY/PHOTOTAKE

The head of a dog tick, *Dermacentor variabilis*, enlarged and colorized for effect.

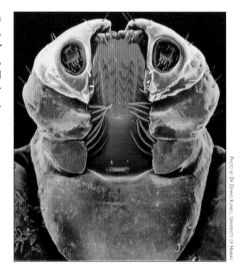

PHOTO BY DR DENNIS KUNKEL, UNIVERSITY OF HAWAII

have life expectancies of a week to six months, depending upon climatic conditions. They can neither jump nor fly, but they can crawl slowly and can range up to 5 metres (16 feet) to reach a sleeping or unsuspecting dog.

MANGE

Mites cause a skin irritation called mange. Some mites are contagious, like *Cheyletiella*, ear mites, scabies and chiggers. Mites that infest ears are usually controlled with Lindane,

Human lice look like dog lice; the two are closely related.

PHOTO BY DWIGHT R KUHN

DEER-TICK CROSSING

The great outdoors may be fun for your dog, but it also is an home to dangerous ticks. Deer ticks carry a bacterium known as *Borrelia burgdorferi* and are most active in the autumn and spring. When infections are caught early, penicillin and tetracycline are effective antibiotics, but if left untreated the bacteria may cause neurological, kidney and cardiac problems as well as long-term trouble with walking and painful joints.

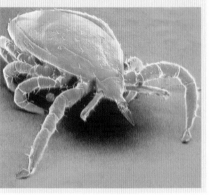

S. E. M. BY DR ANDREW SPIELMAN/PHOTOTAKE

which can only be administered by a vet, followed by Tresaderm at home. It is essential that your dog be treated for mange as quickly as possible because some forms of mange are transmissible to people.

Opposite page:
The dog tick, *Dermacentor variabilis*, is probably the most common tick found on dogs. Look at the strength in its eight legs! No wonder it's hard to detach them.

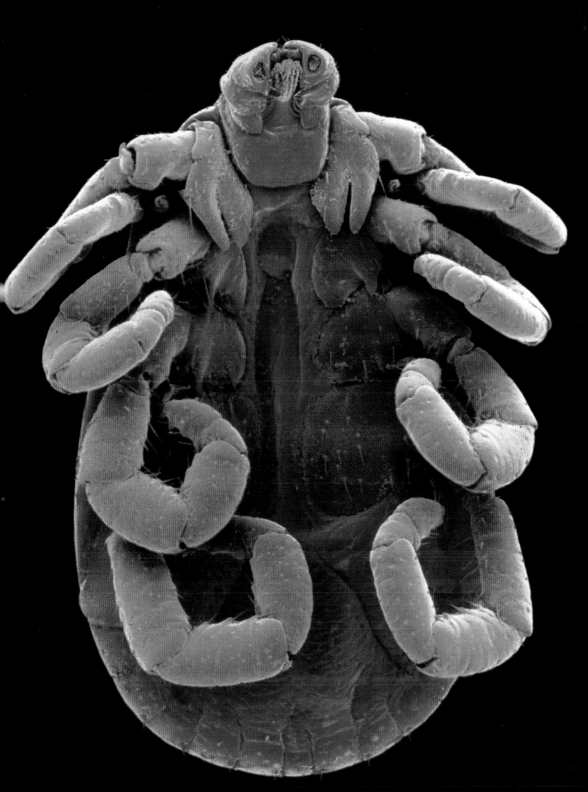

The mange mite,
Psoroptes bovis.

INTERNAL PARASITES

Most animals—fishes, birds and mammals, including dogs and humans—have worms and other parasites that live inside their bodies. According to Dr Herbert R Axelrod, the fish pathologist, there are two kinds of parasites: dumb and smart. The smart parasites live in peaceful cooperation with their hosts (symbiosis), while the dumb parasites kill their hosts. Most worm infections are relatively easy to control. If they are not controlled, they weaken the host dog to the point that other medical problems occur, but they do not kill the host as dumb parasites would.

ROUNDWORMS

The roundworms that infect dogs are known scientifically as *Toxocara canis*. They live in the dog's intestines and shed eggs continually. It has been estimated that a dog produces about 150 grammes of faeces every day. Each gramme of faeces averages 10,000–12,000 eggs of roundworms. There are no known areas in which dogs roam that do not contain roundworm eggs. The greatest danger of roundworms is

ROUNDWORMS

Average-size dogs can pass 1,360,000 roundworm eggs every day. For example, if there were only 1 million dogs in the world, the world would be saturated with 1,300 metric tonnes of dog faeces. These faeces would contain 15,000,000,000 roundworm eggs.

Up to 31% of home gardens and children's play boxes in the US contain roundworm eggs.

Flushing dog's faeces down the toilet is not a safe practice because the usual sewage treatments do not destroy roundworm eggs.

Infected puppies start shedding roundworm eggs at 3 weeks of age. They can be infected by their mother's milk.

PHOTO BY CAROLINA BIOLOGICAL SUPPLY/PHOTOTAKE

The roundworm *Rhabditis* can infect both dogs and humans.

that they infect people too! It is wise to have your dog tested regularly for roundworms.

Pigs also have roundworm infections that can be passed to humans and dogs. The typical roundworm parasite is called *Ascaris lumbricoides.*

DEWORMING

Ridding your puppy of worms is *very important* because certain worms that puppies carry, such as tapeworms and roundworms, can infect humans.

Breeders initiate deworming programmes at or about four weeks of age. The routine is repeated every two or three weeks until the puppy is three months old. The breeder from whom you obtained your puppy should provide you with the complete details of the deworming programme.

Your veterinary surgeon can prescribe and monitor the programme of deworming for you. The usual programme is treating the puppy every 15–20 days until the puppy is positively worm-free. It is advised that you only treat your puppy with drugs that are recommended professionally.

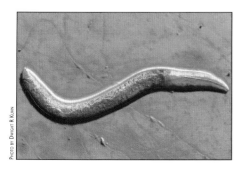

PHOTO BY DWIGHT R KUHN

The common roundworm, *Ascaris lumbricoides.*

Left: *Ancylostoma caninum* are uncommonly found in pet or show dogs in Britain.

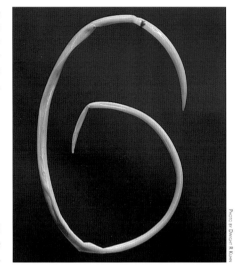

Right: Male and female hookworms.

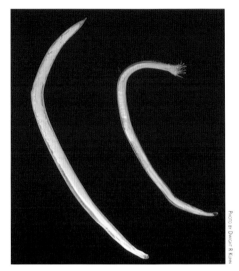

The infective stage of the hookworm larva.

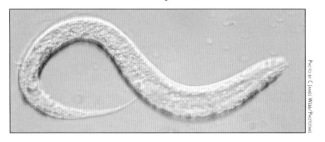

HOOKWORMS

The worm *Ancylostoma caninum* is commonly called the dog hookworm. It is also dangerous to humans and cats. It has teeth by which it attaches itself to the intestines of the dog. It changes the site of its attachment about six times a day and the dog loses blood from each detachment, possibly causing iron-deficiency anaemia. Hookworms are easily purged from the dog with many medications. Milbemycin oxime, which also serves as an heartworm preventative in Collies, can be used for this purpose.

In Britain, the 'temperate climate' hookworm (*Uncinaria stenocephala*) is rarely found in pet or show dogs, but can occur in hunting packs, racing Greyhounds and sheepdogs because the worms can be prevalent wherever dogs are exercised regularly on grassland.

TAPEWORMS

There are many species of tapeworm, all of which are carried by fleas! The dog eats the flea and starts the tapeworm cycle. Humans can also be infected with tapeworms—so don't eat fleas! Fleas are so small that your dog could pass them onto your hands, your plate or your food and thus make it possible for you to ingest a flea that is carrying tapeworm eggs.

TAPEWORMS

Humans, rats, squirrels, foxes, coyotes, wolves and domestic dogs are all susceptible to tapeworm infection. Except in humans, tapeworms are usually not a fatal infection. Infected individuals can harbour 1000 parasitic worms.

Tapeworms, like some other types of worm, are hermaphroditic, meaning male and female in the same worm.

If dogs eat infected rats or mice, they get the tapeworm disease. One month after attaching to a dog's intestine, the worm starts shedding eggs. These eggs are infective immediately. Infective eggs can live for a few months without an host animal.

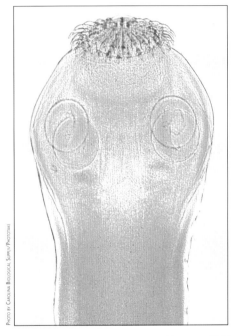

The head and rostellum (the round prominence on the scolex) of a tapeworm, which infects dogs and humans.

PHOTO BY CAROLINA BIOLOGICAL SUPPLY/PHOTOTAKE

While tapeworm infection is not life-threatening in dogs (smart parasite!), it can be the cause of a very serious liver disease for humans. About 50 percent of the humans infected with *Echinococcus multilocularis*, a type of tapeworm that causes alveolar hydatis, perish.

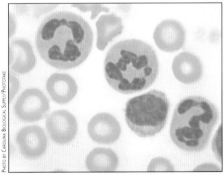

Magnified heartworm larvae, *Dirofilaria immitis.*

PHOTO BY CAROLINA BIOLOGICAL SUPPLY/PHOTOTAKE

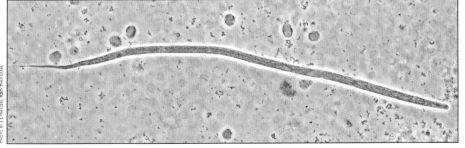

Heartworm, *Dirofilaria immitis.*

PHOTO BY J E HAYDEN, RBP/PHOTOTAKE

First Aid at a Glance

Burns
Place the affected area under cool water; use ice if only a small area is burnt.

Insect bites
Apply ice to relieve swelling; antihistamine dosed properly.

Animal bites
Clean any bleeding area; apply pressure until bleeding subsides; go to the vet.

Spider bites
Use cold compress and a pressurised pack to inhibit venom's spreading.

Antifreeze poisoning
Induce vomiting with hydrogen peroxide. Seek *immediate* veterinary help!

Fish hooks
Removal best handled by vet; hook must be cut in order to remove.

Snake bites
Pack ice around bite; contact vet quickly; identify snake for proper antivenin.

Road-traffic accident
Move dog from roadway with blanket; seek veterinary aid.

Shock
Calm the dog, keep him warm; seek immediate veterinary help.

Nosebleed
Apply cold compress to the nose; apply pressure to any visible abrasion.

Bleeding
Apply pressure above the area; treat wound by applying a cotton pack.

Heat stroke
Submerge dog in cold bath; cool down with fresh air and water; go to the vet.

Frostbite/Hypothermia
Warm the dog with a warm bath, electric blankets or hot water bottles.

Abrasions
Clean the wound and wash out thoroughly with fresh water; apply antiseptic.

 Remember: an injured dog may attempt to bite an helping hand from fear and confusion. Always muzzle the dog before trying to offer assistance.

HEARTWORMS

Heartworms are thin, extended worms up to 30 cms (12 ins) long, which live in a dog's heart and the major blood vessels surrounding it. Dogs may have up to 200 worms. Symptoms may be loss of energy, loss of appetite, coughing, the development of a pot belly and anaemia.

Heartworms are transmitted by mosquitoes. The mosquito drinks the blood of an infected dog and takes in larvae with the blood. The larvae, called microfilaria, develop within the body of the mosquito and are passed on to the next dog bitten after the larvae mature. It takes two to three weeks for the larvae to develop to the infective stage within the body of the mosquito. Dogs should be treated at about six weeks of age, and maintained on a prophylactic dose given monthly.

Blood testing for heartworms is not necessarily indicative of how seriously your dog is infected. This is a dangerous disease. Although heartworm is a problem for dogs in America, Australia, Asia and Central Europe, dogs in the United Kingdom currently are not affected by heartworm.

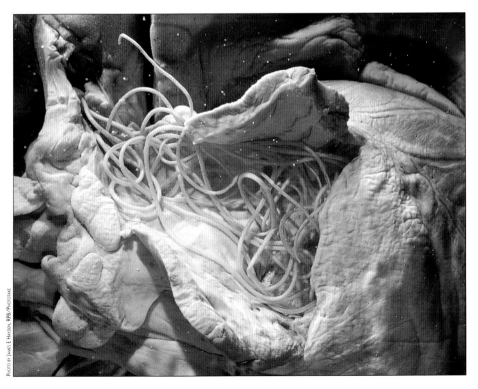

The heart of a dog infected with canine heartworm, *Dirofilaria immitis.*

PHOTO BY JAMES E HAYDEN, RPB/PHOTOTAKE

HOMEOPATHY:
an alternative
to conventional
medicine

'Less is Most'

Using this principle, the strength of an homeopathic remedy is measured by the number of serial dilutions that were undertaken to create it. The greater the number of serial dilutions, the greater the strength of the homeopathic remedy. The potency of a remedy that has been made by making a dilution of 1 part in 100 parts (or 1/100) is 1c or 1cH. If this remedy is subjected to a series of further dilutions, each one being 1/100, a more dilute and stronger remedy is produced. If the remedy is diluted in this way six times, it is called 6c or 6cH. A dilution of 6c is 1 part in 1,000,000,000,000. In general, higher potencies in more frequent doses are better for acute symptoms and lower potencies in more infrequent doses are more useful for chronic, long-standing problems.

CURING OUR DOGS NATURALLY

Holistic medicine means treating the whole animal as a unique, perfect living being. Generally, holistic treatments do not suppress the symptoms that the body naturally produces, as do most medications prescribed by conventional doctors and vets. Holistic methods seek to cure disease by regaining balance and harmony in the patient's environment. Some of these methods include use of nutritional therapy, herbs, flower essences, aromatherapy, acupuncture, massage, chiropractic and, of course, the most popular holistic approach, homeopathy.

Homeopathy is a theory or system of treating illness with small doses of substances which, if administered in larger quantities, would produce the symptoms that the patient already has. This approach is often described as 'like cures like.' Although modern veterinary medicine is geared toward the 'quick fix,' homeopathy relies on the belief that, given the time, the body is able to heal itself and return to its natural, healthy state.

Choosing a remedy to cure a problem in our dogs is the difficult part of homeopathy. Consult with your veterinary surgeon for a professional diagnosis of your dog's symptoms. Often these symptoms require immediate conventional care. If your vet is willing, and knowledgeable, you may attempt an homeopathic remedy. Be aware that cortisone prevents homeopathic remedies from working. There are hundreds of possibilities and combinations to cure many problems in dogs, from basic physical problems such as excessive moulting, fleas or other parasites, unattractive doggy odour, bad breath, upset tummy, obesity,

dry, oily or dull coat, diarrhoea, ear problems or eye discharge (including tears and dry or mucousy matter), to behavioural abnormalities such as fear of loud noises, habitual licking, poor appetite, excessive barking and various phobias. From alumina to zincum metallicum, the remedies span the planet and the imagination…from flowers and weeds to chemicals, insect droppings, diesel smoke and volcanic ash.

Using 'Like to Treat Like'

Unlike conventional medicines that suppress symptoms, homeopathic remedies treat illnesses with small doses of substances that, if administered in larger quantities, would produce the symptoms that the patient already has. While the same homeopathic remedy can be used to treat different symptoms in different dogs, here are some interesting remedies and their uses.

Apis Mellifica
(made from honey bee venom) can be used for allergies or to reduce swelling that occurs in acutely infected kidneys.

Diesel Smoke
can be used to help control travel sickness.

Calcarea Fluorica
(made from calcium fluoride, which helps harden bone structure) can be useful in treating hard lumps in tissues.

Natrum Muriaticum
(made from common salt, sodium chloride) is useful in treating thin, thirsty dogs.

Nitricum Acidum
(made from nitric acid) is used for symptoms you would expect to see from contact with acids, such as lesions, especially where the skin joins the linings of body orifices or openings such as the lips and nostrils.

Symphytum
(made from the herb Knitbone, *Symphytum officianale*) is used to encourage bones to heal.

Urtica Urens
(made from the common stinging nettle) is used in treating painful, irritating rashes.

HOMEOPATHIC REMEDIES FOR YOUR DOG

Symptom/Ailment	Possible Remedy
ALLERGIES	Apis Mellifica 30c, Astacus Fluviatilis 6c, Pulsatilla 30c, Urtica Urens 6c
ALOPAECIA	Alumina 30c, Lycopodium 30c, Sepia 30c, Thallium 6c
ANAL GLANDS (BLOCKED)	Hepar Sulphuris Calcareum 30c, Sanicula 6c, Silicea 6c
ARTHRITIS	Rhus Toxicodendron 6c, Bryonia Alba 6c
CATARACT	Calcarea Carbonica 6c, Conium Maculatum 6c, Phosphorus 30c, Silicea 30c
CONSTIPATION	Alumina 6c, Carbo Vegetabilis 30c, Graphites 6c, Nitricum Acidum 30c, Silicea 6c
COUGHING	Aconitum Napellus 6c, Belladonna 30c, Hyoscyamus Niger 30c, Phosphorus 30c
DIARRHOEA	Arsenicum Album 30c, Aconitum Napellus 6c, Chamomilla 30c, Mercurius Corrosivus 30c
DRY EYE	Zincum Metallicum 30c
EAR PROBLEMS	Aconitum Napellus 30c, Belladonna 30c, Hepar Sulphuris 30c, Tellurium 30c, Psorinum 200c
EYE PROBLEMS	Borax 6c, Aconitum Napellus 30c, Graphites 6c, Staphysagria 6c, Thuja Occidentalis 30c
GLAUCOMA	Aconitum Napellus 30c, Apis Mellifica 6c, Phosphorus 30c
HEAT STROKE	Belladonna 30c, Gelsemium Sempervirens 30c, Sulphur 30c
HICCOUGHS	Cinchona Deficinalis 6c
HIP DYSPLASIA	Colocynthis 6c, Rhus Toxicodendron 6c, Bryonia Alba 6c
INCONTINENCE	Argentum Nitricum 6c, Causticum 30c, Conium Maculatum 30c, Pulsatilla 30c, Sepia 30c
INSECT BITES	Apis Mellifica 30c, Cantharis 30c, Hypericum Perforatum 6c, Urtica Urens 30c
ITCHING	Alumina 30c, Arsenicum Album 30c, Carbo Vegetabilis 30c, Hypericum Perforatum 6c, Mezerium 6c, Sulphur 30c
KENNEL COUGH	Drosera 6c, Ipecacuanha 30c
MASTITIS	Apis Mellifica 30c, Belladonna 30c, Urtica Urens 1m
PATELLAR LUXATION	Gelsemium Sempervirens 6c, Rhus Toxicodendron 6c
PENIS PROBLEMS	Aconitum Napellus 30c, Hepar Sulphuris Calcareum 30c, Pulsatilla 30c, Thuja Occidentalis 6c
PUPPY TEETHING	Calcarea Carbonica 6c, Chamomilla 6c, Phytolacca 6c
TRAVEL SICKNESS	Cocculus 6c, Petroleum 6c

Recognising a Sick Dog

Unlike colicky babies and cranky children, our canine charges cannot tell us when they are feeling ill. Therefore, there are a number of signs that owners can identify to know that their dogs are not feeling well.

Take note for physical manifestations such as:

- unusual, bad odour, including bad breath
- excessive moulting
- wax in the ears, chronic ear irritation
- oily, flaky, dull haircoat
- mucous, tearing or similar discharge in the eyes
- fleas or mites
- mucous in stool, diarrhoea
- sensitivity to petting or handling
- licking at paws, scratching face, etc.

Keep an eye out for behavioural changes as well including:

- lethargy, idleness
- lack of patience or general irritability
- lack of appetite, digestive problems
- phobias (fear of people, loud noises, etc.)
- strange behaviour, suspicion, fear
- coprophagia
- more frequent barking
- whimpering, crying

Get Well Soon

You don't need a DVR or a BVMA to provide good TLC to your sick or recovering dog, but you do need to pay attention to some details that normally wouldn't bother him. The following tips will aid Fido's recovery and get him back on his paws again:

- Keep his space free of irritating smells, like heavy perfumes and air fresheners.
- Rest is the best medicine! Avoid harsh lighting that will prevent your dog from sleeping. Shade him from bright sunlight during the day and dim the lights in the evening.
- Keep the noise level down. Animals are more sensitive to sound when they are sick.

- Be attentive to any necessary temperature adjustments. A dog with a fever needs a cool room and cold liquids. A bitch that is whelping or recovering from surgery will be more comfortable in a warm room, consuming warm liquids and food.
- You wouldn't send a sick child back to school early, so don't rush your dog back into a full routine until he seems absolutely ready.

Number-One Killer Disease in Dogs: CANCER

In every age, there is a word associated with a disease or plague that causes humans to shudder. In the 21st century, that word is 'cancer.' Just as cancer is the leading cause of death in humans, it claims nearly half the lives of dogs that die from a natural disease as well as half the dogs that die over the age of ten years.

Described as a genetic disease, cancer becomes a greater risk as the dog ages. Veterinary surgeons and dog owners have become increasingly aware of the threat of cancer to dogs. Statistics reveal that one dog in every five will develop cancer, the most common of which is skin cancer. Many cancers, including prostate, ovarian and breast cancer, can be avoided by spaying and neutering our dogs by the age of six months.

Early detection of cancer can save or extend your dog's life, so it is absolutely vital for owners to have their dogs examined by a qualified veterinary surgeon or oncologist immediately upon detection of any abnormality. Certain dietary guidelines have also proven to reduce the onset and spread of cancer. Foods based on fish rather than beef, due to the presence of Omega-3 fatty acids, are recommended. Other amino acids such as glutamine have significant benefits for canines, particularly those breeds that show a greater susceptibility to cancer.

Cancer management and treatments promise hope for future generations of canines. Since the disease is genetic, breeders should never breed a dog whose parents, grandparents or any related siblings have developed cancer. It is difficult to know whether to exclude an otherwise healthy dog from a breeding programme as the disease does not manifest itself until the dog's senior years.

RECOGNISE CANCER WARNING SIGNS

Since early detection can possibly rescue your dog from becoming a cancer statistic, it is essential for owners to recognise the possible signs and seek the assistance of a qualified professional.

- Abnormal bumps or lumps that continue to grow
- Bleeding or discharge from any body cavity
- Persistent stiffness or lameness
- Recurrent sores or sores that do not heal
- Inappetence
- Breathing difficulties
- Weight loss
- Bad breath or odours
- General malaise and fatigue
- Eating and swallowing problems
- Difficulty urinating and defecating

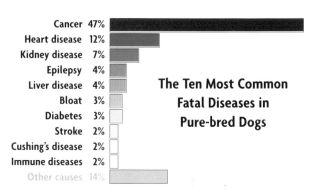

Disease	Percentage
Cancer	47%
Heart disease	12%
Kidney disease	7%
Epilepsy	4%
Liver disease	4%
Bloat	3%
Diabetes	3%
Stroke	2%
Cushing's disease	2%
Immune diseases	2%
Other causes	14%

The Ten Most Common Fatal Diseases in Pure-bred Dogs

KING CHARLES SPANIEL

The term *old* is a qualitative term. For dogs, as well as for their masters, old is relative. Certainly we can all distinguish between a puppy King Charles Spaniel and an adult King Charles Spaniel—there are the obvious physical traits, such as size, appearance and facial expressions, and personality traits. Puppies and young dogs like to play with children. Children's natural exuberance is a good match for the seemingly endless energy of young dogs. They like to run, jump, chase and retrieve. When dogs grow older and cease their interaction with children, they are often thought of as being too old to keep pace with the kids. On the other hand, if a King Charles Spaniel is only exposed to older people or quieter lifestyles, his life will normally be less active and the decrease in his activity level as he ages will not be as obvious.

If people live to be 100 years old, dogs live to be 20 years old. While this might seem like a good rule of thumb, it is very inaccurate. When trying to compare dog years to human years, you cannot make a generalisation about all dogs. You can make the generalisation that 10 to 15 years is a good lifespan for a King Charles Spaniel. Dogs generally are considered physically mature at three years of age (or earlier), but can reproduce even earlier. The King Charles reaches full height as early as one year, though takes another year to develop completely.

Usually, the first three years of a dog's life are like seven times that of comparable humans. That means a 3-year-old dog is like a 21-year-old human. As the curve of comparison shows, there is no hard and fast rule for comparing dog and human ages. Small breeds tend to live longer than large breeds, some breeds' adolescent periods last longer than others' and some breeds experience rapid periods of growth. The comparison is made even more difficult, for, likewise, not all humans age at the same rate...and human females live longer than human males.

WHAT TO LOOK FOR

Most veterinary surgeons and behaviourists use the seven-year mark as the time to consider a dog a 'senior' or 'veteran.' Neither term implies that the dog is geriatric and has begun to fail in mind and body. Ageing is essentially a slowing process. Humans readily admit that they feel a difference in their activity level from age 20 to 30, and then from 30 to 40, etc. By treating the seven-year-old dog as a senior, owners are able to implement certain therapeutic and preventative medical strategies with the help of their veterinary surgeons.

A senior-care programme should include at least two veterinary visits per year and screening sessions to determine the dog's health status, as well as nutritional counselling.

Veterinary surgeons determine the senior dog's health status through a blood smear for a complete blood count, serum chemistry profile with electrolytes, urinalysis, blood pressure check, electrocardiogram, ocular tonometry (pressure on the eyeball) and dental prophylaxis.

Such an extensive programme for senior dogs is well advised before owners start to see the obvious physical signs of ageing, such as slower and inhibited movement, greying, increased sleep/nap periods and disinterest in play and other activity. This preventative programme promises a longer, healthier life for the ageing dog. Among the physical problems

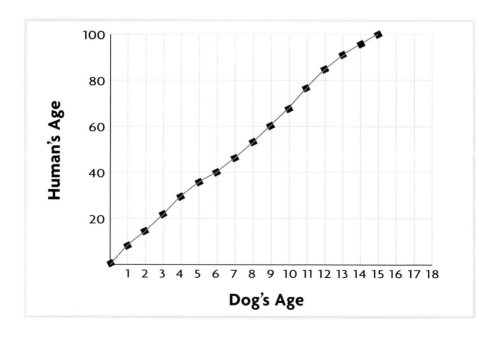

CDS: COGNITIVE DYSFUNCTION SYNDROME
'OLD-DOG SYNDROME'

There are many ways to evaluate old-dog syndrome. Veterinary surgeons have defined CDS (cognitive dysfunction syndrome) as the gradual deterioration of cognitive abilities. These are indicated by changes in the dog's behaviour. When a dog changes its routine response, and maladies have been eliminated as the cause of these behavioural changes, then CDS is the usual diagnosis.

More than half the dogs over eight years old suffer from some form of CDS. The older the dog, the more chance it has of suffering from CDS. In humans, doctors often dismiss the CDS behavioural changes as part of 'winding down.'

There are four major signs of CDS: the dog has frequent toilet accidents inside the home, sleeps much more or much less than normal, acts confused and fails to respond to social stimuli.

SYMPTOMS OF CDS

FREQUENT TOILET ACCIDENTS
- *Urinates in the house.*
- *Defecates in the house.*
- *Doesn't signal that he wants to go out.*

SLEEP PATTERNS
- *Moves much more slowly.*
- *Sleeps more than normal during the day.*
- *Sleeps less during the night.*

CONFUSION
- *Goes outside and just stands there.*
- *Appears confused with a faraway look in his eyes.*
- *Hides more often.*
- *Doesn't recognise friends.*
- *Doesn't come when called.*
- *Walks around listlessly and without a destination.*

FAILS TO RESPOND TO SOCIAL STIMULI
- *Comes to people less frequently, whether called or not.*
- *Doesn't tolerate petting for more than a short time.*
- *Doesn't come to the door when you return home.*

common in ageing dogs are the loss of sight and hearing, arthritis, kidney and liver failure, diabetes mellitus, heart disease and Cushing's disease (an hormonal disease).

GETTING OLD

The bottom line is simply that your dog is getting old when YOU think he is getting old because he slows down in his level of general activity, including walking, running, eating, jumping and retrieving. On the other hand, the frequency of certain activities increases, such as more sleeping, more barking and more repetition of habits like going to the door without being called when you put your coat on to leave the house.

CONSISTENCY COUNTS

Puppies and older dogs are very similar in their need for consistency in their lives. Older pets may experience hearing and vision loss, or may just be more easily confused by changes in their homes. Try to keep things consistent for the senior dog. For example, doors that are always open or closed should remain so. Most importantly, don't dismiss a pet just because he's getting old; most senior dogs remain active and important parts of their owners' lives.

In addition to the physical manifestations discussed, there are some behavioural changes and problems related to ageing dogs. Dogs suffering from hearing or vision loss, dental discomfort or arthritis can become aggressive. Likewise, the near-deaf and/or blind dog may be startled more easily and react in an unexpectedly aggressive manner. Seniors suffering from senility can become more impatient and irritable. Housesoiling accidents are associated with loss of mobility, kidney problems and loss of sphincter control as well as plaque accumulation, physiological brain changes and reactions to medications. Older dogs, just like young puppies, suffer from separation anxiety, which can lead to excessive barking, whining, housesoiling

KEEPING SENIORS WARM

The coats of many older dogs become thinner as they age, which makes them more sensitive to cold temperatures and more susceptible to illness. During cold weather, limit time spent outdoors and be extremely cautious with any artificial sources of warmth such as heat lamps, as these can cause severe burns. Your old-timer may need a jumper to wear over his coat.

puts additional stress on the body's vital organs. Some breeders recommend supplementing the diet with foods high in fibre and lower in calories. Adding fresh vegetables and marrow broth to the senior's diet makes a tasty, low-calorie, low-fat supplement. Vets also offer speciality diets for senior dogs

and destructive behaviour. Seniors may become fearful of everyday sounds, such as vacuum cleaners, heaters, thunder and passing traffic. Some dogs have difficulty sleeping, due to discomfort, the need for frequent toilet visits and the like.

Owners should avoid spoiling the older dog with too many fatty treats. Obesity is a common problem in older dogs and subtracts years from their lives. Keep the senior dog as trim as possible, since excessive weight

SENIOR SIGNS

An old dog starts to show one or more of the following symptoms:

- The hair on the face and paws starts to turn grey. The colour breakdown usually starts around the eyes and mouth.
- Sleep patterns are deeper and longer, and the old dog is harder to awaken.
- Food intake diminishes.
- Responses to calls, whistles and other signals are ignored more and more.
- Eye contact does not evoke tail wagging (assuming it once did).

AGEING ADDITIVES

An healthy diet is important for dogs of all ages, but older dogs may benefit from the addition of supplements like antioxidants, which fight the ageing process, and vitamin B, which aids the kidneys. Check with your vet before adding these or any supplements to your pet's diet.

that are worth exploring.

Your dog, as he nears his twilight years, needs your patience and good care more than ever. Never punish an older dog for an accident or abnormal behaviour. For all the years of love and companionship that your dog has provided, he deserves special attention and

NOTICING THE SYMPTOMS

The symptoms listed below are symptoms that gradually appear and become more noticeable. They are not life-threatening; however, the symptoms below are to be taken very seriously and warrant a discussion with your veterinary surgeon:

- Your dog cries and whimpers when he moves, and he stops running completely.

- Convulsions start or become more serious and frequent. The usual convulsion (spasm) is when the dog stiffens and starts to tremble, being unable or unwilling to move. The seizure usually lasts for 5 to 30 minutes.

- Your dog drinks more water and urinates more frequently. Wetting and bowel accidents take place indoors without warning.

- Vomiting becomes more and more frequent.

courtesies. The older dog may need to relieve himself at 3 a.m. because he can no longer 'hold it' for eight hours. Older dogs may not be able to remain crated for more than two or three hours. It may be time to give up a sofa or chair to your old friend. Although he may not seem as enthusiastic about your attention and petting, he does appreciate the considerations you offer as he gets older.

Your King Charles Spaniel does not understand why his world is slowing down. Owners must make their dogs' transition into their golden years as pleasant and rewarding as possible.

WHAT TO DO WHEN THE TIME COMES

You are never fully prepared to make a rational decision about putting your dog to sleep. It is very obvious that you love your King Charles Spaniel or you would not be reading this book. Putting a beloved dog to sleep is extremely difficult. It is a decision that must be made with your veterinary surgeon. You are usually forced to make the decision when your dog experiences one or more life-threatening symptoms that have become serious enough for you to seek medical (veterinary) help.

If the prognosis of the malady indicates that the end is near and that your beloved pet will only continue to suffer and experience no enjoyment for the balance of its life, then euthanasia is the right choice.

EUTHANASIA SERVICES

Euthanasia must be performed by a licenced veterinary surgeon. There also may be societies for the prevention of cruelty to animals in your area. They often offer this service upon a vet's recommendation.

TALK IT OUT
The more openly your family discusses the whole stressful occurrence of the ageing and eventual loss of a beloved pet, the easier it will be for you when the time comes.

Many pet cemeteries have facilities for storing a dog's ashes.

WHAT IS EUTHANASIA?

Euthanasia derives from the Greek, meaning *good death*. In other words, it means the planned, painless killing of a dog suffering from a painful, incurable condition, or who is so aged that it cannot walk, see, eat or control its excretory functions. Euthanasia is usually accomplished by injection with an overdose of anaesthesia or a barbiturate. Aside from the prick of the needle, the experience is usually painless.

MAKING THE DECISION

The decision to euthanise your dog is never easy. The days during which the dog becomes ill and the end occurs can be unusually stressful for you. If this is your first experience with the death of a loved one, you may need the comfort dictated by your religious beliefs. If you are the head of the family and have children, you should have involved them in the decision of putting your King Charles Spaniel to sleep. Usually your dog can be maintained on drugs for a few days in order to give you ample time to make a

Consult your veterinary surgeon to help you locate a pet cemetery in your area.

COPING WITH LOSS

When your dog dies, you may be as upset as when a human companion passes away. You are losing your chum, your baby, your confidante and your best friend. Many people experience not only grief but also feelings of guilt and doubt as to whether they did all that they could for their pet. Allow yourself to grieve and mourn, and seek help from friends and support groups. You may also wish to consult books and websites that deal with this topic.

decision. During this time, talking with members of your family or with people who have lived through the same experience can ease the burden of your inevitable decision.

THE FINAL RESTING PLACE

Dogs can have some of the same privileges as humans. The remains of your beloved dog can be buried in a pet cemetery, which is generally expensive. Alternatively, your dog can be cremated individually and the ashes returned to you. A less expensive option is mass cremation, although, of course, the ashes cannot then be returned. Vets can usually arrange the cremation on your behalf. The cost of these options should always be discussed

frankly and openly with your veterinary surgeon. In Britain, if your dog has died at the surgery, the vet legally cannot allow you to take your dog's body home, as home garden burials are not permitted.

GETTING ANOTHER DOG?

The grief of losing your beloved dog will be as lasting as the grief of losing a human friend or relative. In most cases, if your dog died of old age (if there is such a thing), it had slowed down considerably. Do you want a new King Charles Spaniel puppy to replace it? Or are you better off finding a more mature King Charles Spaniel, say two to three years of age, which will usually be house-trained and will have an already developed personality. In this case, you can find out if you like each other after a few hours of being together.

The decision is, of course, your own. Do you want another King Charles Spaniel or perhaps a different breed so as to avoid comparison with your beloved friend? Most people usually buy the same breed because they know (and love) the characteristics of that breed. Then, too, they often know people who have the same breed and perhaps they are lucky enough that one of their friends expects a litter soon. What could be better?

Showing Your

KING CHARLES SPANIEL

HOW TO ENTER A DOG SHOW

To enter a dog show in Britain, you need to look at one of the two dog papers, which come out on Fridays and can be ordered at any newsagent. Find the phone number of the secretary of a show, and call to obtain a timetable and entry form. Fill in the form with the classes you wish to enter (double-check your form!) and do not forget to send a cheque for the entries. Show entries close six weeks or so before the show.

You cannot enter a conformation show if your dog is not registered with The Kennel Club. If you have sent off the forms to The Kennel Club to transfer the dog into your name, it is possible to enter with 'TAF' (transfer applied for) after the dog's name.

When you purchase your King Charles Spaniel, you will make it clear to the breeder whether you want one just as a loveable companion and pet, or if you hope to be buying a King Charles Spaniel with show prospects. No reputable breeder will sell you a young puppy and tell you that it is *definitely* of show quality, for so much can go wrong during the early months of a puppy's development. If you plan to show, what you will hopefully have acquired is a puppy with 'show potential.'

What to do at an outdoor show on a rainy day? Wonder no more...

WINNING THE TICKET

Earning a championship at Kennel Club shows is the most difficult in the world. Compared to the United States and Canada, where it is relatively not 'challenging,' collecting three green tickets not only requires much time and effort, it can be very expensive! Challenge Certificates, as the tickets are properly known, are the building blocks of champions—good breeding, good handling, good training and good luck!

To the novice, exhibiting a King Charles Spaniel in the show ring may look easy, but it takes a lot of hard work and devotion to do top winning at a show such as the prestigious Crufts Dog Show, not to mention a little luck too!

The first concept that the canine novice learns when watching a dog show is that each dog first competes against members of its own breed. Once the judge has selected the best member of each breed (Best of Breed), provided that the show is judged on a Group system, that chosen dog will compete with other dogs in its group. Finally, the best of each group will compete for Best in Show and Reserve Best in Show.

The second concept that you must understand is that the dogs are not actually compared against one another. The judge compares each dog against its breed standard, which is the written description of the ideal specimen of the breed. While some early breed standards were indeed based on specific dogs that were famous or popular, many dedicated enthusiasts say that a perfect specimen, as described in the standard, has never walked into a show ring, has never been bred and, to the woe of dog breeders around the globe, does not exist. Breeders attempt to get as close to this ideal as possible with every litter, but theoretically the 'perfect' dog is so elusive that it is impossible. (And if the 'perfect' dog were born, breeders and judges would probably never agree that it was indeed 'perfect.')

If you are interested in exploring the world of dog showing, your best bet is to join your local breed club. These clubs often host both Championship and Open Shows, and sometimes Match meetings and special events, all of which could be of interest, even if you are only an onlooker. Clubs also send out newsletters, and some organise training days and seminars in order that people may learn more about their chosen breed.

To locate the breed club closest to you, contact The Kennel Club, the ruling body for the British dog world. The Kennel Club governs not only conformation shows but also working trials, obedience shows, agility trials and field trials. The Kennel Club furnishes the rules and regulations for all of these events plus general dog registration and other basic requirements of dog ownership. Its annual show, called the Crufts Dog Show, held in Birmingham, is the largest benched show in England. Every year over 20,000 of the UK's best dogs qualify to participate in this marvellous show, which lasts four days.

The Kennel Club governs many different kinds of shows in

INFORMATION ON CLUBS

You can get information about dog shows from the national kennel clubs:

The Kennel Club
1-5 Clarges St., Piccadilly, London W1Y 8AB
UK
www.the-kennel-club.org.uk

Fédération Cynologique Internationale
14, rue Leopold II, B-6530 Thuin, Belgium
www.fci.be

American Kennel Club
5580 Centerview Dr., Raleigh, NC 27606-3390
USA
www.akc.org

Canadian Kennel Club
89 Skyway Ave., Suite 100, Etobicoke, Ontario
M9W 6R4 Canada
www.ckc.ca

TIDINESS COUNTS

Surely you've spent hours grooming your dog to perfection for the show ring, but don't forget about yourself! While the dog should be the centre of attention, it is important that you also appear clean and tidy. Wear smart, appropriate clothes and comfortable shoes in a colour that contrasts with your dog's coat. Look and act like a professional.

Great Britain, Australia, South Africa and beyond. At the most competitive and prestigious of these shows, the Championship Shows, a dog can earn Challenge Certificates (CCs), and thereby become a Show Champion or a Champion. A dog must earn three CCs under three different judges to earn the prefix of 'Sh Ch' or 'Ch.' Some breeds must also qualify in a field trial in order to gain the title of full Champion, though the King Charles Spaniel is not one such breed. CCs are awarded to a very small percentage of the dogs competing, and dogs that are already Champions compete with others for these coveted CCs. The number of CCs awarded in any one year is based upon the total number of dogs in each breed entered for competition.

There are three types of Championship Shows: an all-breed General Championship Show for all Kennel-Club-recognised breeds; a Group Championship Show, which is limited to breeds within one of the groups; and a Breed Show, which is usually confined to a single breed. The Kennel Club determines which breeds at which Championship Shows will have the opportunity to earn Challenge Certificates (or tickets). Serious exhibitors often will opt not to participate if the tickets are withheld at a particular show.

This policy makes earning championships even more difficult to accomplish.

Open Shows are generally less competitive and are frequently used as 'practice shows' for young dogs. There are hundreds of Open Shows each year that can be delightful social events and are great first show experiences for the novice. Even if you're considering just watching a show to wet your paws, an Open Show is a great choice.

While Championship and Open Shows are most important for the beginner to understand, there are other types of shows in which the interested dog owner can participate. Training clubs sponsor Matches that can be entered on the day of the show for a nominal fee. In these introductory-level exhibitions, two dogs'

A GENTLEMAN'S SPORT

Whether or not your dog wins top honours, showing is a pleasant social event. Sometimes, one may meet a troublemaker or nasty exhibitor, but these people should be ignored and forgotten. In the extremely rare case that someone threatens or harasses you or your dog, you can lodge a complaint with The Kennel Club. This should be done with extreme prudence. Complaints are investigated seriously and should never be filed on a whim.

names are pulled out of an hat and 'matched,' the winner of that match goes on to the next round and eventually only one dog is left undefeated.

Exemption Shows are much more light-hearted affairs with usually only four pedigree classes and several 'fun' classes, all of which can be entered on the day of the show. Exemption Shows are sometimes held in conjunction

Winning brings more than rosettes and recognition. Most important is the owner's pride in his dog and the bond built by practising and competing together.

The World Dog Show for the new millennium took place in Milan, Italy and attracted thousands of dogs and handlers from around the world.

Dog shows are as social as they are competitive, with the dogs' getting the chance to socialise and the owners' meeting others who share a common interest—the King Charles Spaniel.

with small agricultural shows and the proceeds must be given to a charity. Limited Shows are also available in small number. Entry is restricted to members of the club that hosts the show, although one can usually join the club when making an entry.

Before you actually step into the ring, you would be well advised to sit back and observe the judge's ring procedure. If it is your first time in the ring, do not be over-anxious and run to the front of the line. It is much better to stand back and study how the exhibitor in front of you is performing. The judge asks each handler to 'stand' the dog, hopefully showing the dog off to his best advantage. The judge will observe the dog from a distance and from different angles, and approach the dog to check his

teeth, overall structure, alertness and muscle tone, as well as consider how well the dog 'conforms' to the standard. Most importantly, the judge will have the exhibitor move the dog around the ring in some pattern that he or she should specify (another advantage to not going first, but always listen since some judges change their directions— and the judge is always right!). Finally, the judge will give the dog one last look before moving on to the next exhibitor.

If you are not in the top three at your first show, do not be discouraged. Be patient and consistent, and you may eventu-

SHOW QUALITY SHOWS

While you may purchase a puppy in the hope of having a successful career in the show ring, it is impossible to tell, at eight to ten weeks of age, whether your dog will be a contender. Some promising pups end up with minor to serious faults that prevent them from taking home a Best of Breed award, but this certainly does not mean they can't be the best of companions for you and your family. To find out if your potential show dog is show-quality, enter him in a Match to see how a judge evaluates him. You may also take him back to your breeder as he matures to see what he might advise.

ally find yourself in the winning line-up. Remember that the winners were once in your shoes and have devoted many hours and much money to earn the placement. If you find that your dog is losing every time and never getting a nod, it may be time to consider a different dog sport or to just enjoy your King Charles Spaniel as a pet.

Virtually all countries with a recognised speciality breed club (sometimes called a 'parent' club) offer show conformation competition specifically for and among King Charles Spaniels. Under direction of the club, other special events for tracking,

obedience and agility may be offered as well, whether for titling or just for fun.

FÉDÉRATION CYNOLOGIQUE INTERNATIONALE

Established in 1911, the Fédération Cynologique Internationale (FCI) represents the 'world kennel club.' This international body brings uniformity to the breeding, judging and showing of pure-bred dogs. Although the FCI originally included only five European nations: France, Germany, Austria, the Netherlands and Belgium (which remains its headquarters), the organisation today embraces nations on six continents and recognises well over 300 breeds of pure-bred dog.

The FCI sponsors both national and international shows.

TEN GROUPS

FCI-recognised breeds are divided into ten groups:

Group 1: Sheepdogs and Cattledogs (except Swiss Cattledogs)

Group 2: Pinschers and Schnauzers, Molossians, Swiss Mountain Dogs and Swiss Cattledogs

Group 3: Terriers

Group 4: Dachshunds

Group 5: Spitz- and primitive-type dogs

Group 6: Scenthounds and related breeds

Group 7: Pointing dogs

Group 8: Retrievers, Flushing dogs and Water dogs

Group 9: Companion and Toy dogs

Group 10: Sighthounds

Like most toy and other small breeds, the King Charles is put on a table for evaluation by the judge.

FCI INFORMATION

There are 330 breeds recognised by the FCI, and each breed is considered to be 'owned' by a specific country. Each breed standard is a cooperative effort between the breed's country and the FCI's Standards and Scientific Commissions. Judges use these official breed standards at shows held in FCI member countries. One of the functions of the FCI is to update and translate the breed standards into French, English, Spanish and German.

The hosting country determines the judging system and breed standards are always based on the breed's country of origin. Dogs from every country can participate in these impressive canine spectacles, the largest of which is the World Dog Show, hosted in a different country each year.

There are three titles attainable through the FCI: the International Champion, which is the most prestigious; the International Beauty Champion, which is based on aptitude certificates in different countries; and the International Trial Champion, which is based on achievement in obedience trials in different countries. The title of Champion at an FCI show requires a dog to win three CACs (*Certificats d'Aptitude au Championnat*), at regional or club shows under three different judges who are breed specialists. The title of International Champion is gained by winning four CACIBs (*Certificats d'Aptitude au Championnat International de Beauté*), which

are offered only at international shows, with at least a one-year lapse between the first and fourth award.

The FCI is divided into ten groups. At the World Dog Show, the following classes are offered for each breed: Puppy Class (6–9 months), Junior Class (9–18 months), Open Class (15 months or older) and Champion Class. A dog can be awarded a classification of Excellent, Very Good, Good, Sufficient and Not Sufficient. Puppies can be awarded classifications of Very Promising, Promising or Not Promising. Four placements are made in each class. After all classes are judged, a Best of Breed is selected. Other special groups and classes may also be shown. Each exhibitor showing a dog receives a written evaluation from the judge.

Besides the World Dog Show and other all-breed shows, you can exhibit your dog at speciality shows held by different breed clubs. Speciality shows may have their own regulations.

As a King Charles Spaniel owner, you have selected your dog so that you and your loved ones can have a companion, a protector, a friend and a four-legged family member. You invest time, money and effort to care for and train the family's new charge. Of course, this chosen canine behaves perfectly! Well, perfectly like a *dog*.

THINK LIKE A DOG

Dogs do not think like humans, nor do humans think like dogs, though we try. Unfortunately, a dog is incapable of compre-hending how humans think, so the responsibility falls on the owner to adopt a proper canine mindset. Dogs cannot rationalise, and dogs exist in the present moment. Many a dog owner makes the mistake in training of thinking that he can reprimand his dog for something the dog did a while ago. Basically, you cannot even reprimand a dog for something he did 20 seconds ago! Either catch him in the act or forget it! It is a waste of your and your dog's time—in his mind, you are reprimanding him for what-ever he is doing at that moment.

The following behavioural problems represent some which owners most commonly encounter. Every dog is unique and every situation is unique. No author could purport for you to solve your King Charles Spaniel's problems simply by reading a script. Here we outline some basic 'dogspeak' so that owners' chances of solving behavioural problems are increased.

Discuss bad habits with your veterinary surgeon and he/she can recommend a behavioural specialist to consult in appro-priate cases. Since behavioural abnormalities are the main reason for owners' abandoning their pets, we hope that you will make a valiant effort to solve your King Charles Spaniel's problems. Patience and understanding are virtues that must dwell in every pet-loving household.

SEPARATION ANXIETY

Recognised by behaviourists as the most common form of stress for dogs, separation anxiety can also lead to destructive behav-iours in your dog. It's more than your King Charles Spaniel's howling his displeasure at your leaving the house and his being left alone. This is a normal reaction, no different from the child who cries as his mother leaves him on the first day at school. However, separation anxiety is more serious. In fact, if you are constantly with your dog, he will come to expect you with him all of the time, making it even more traumatic for him when you are not there. Obviously, you enjoy spending time with your dog, and he thrives on your love and attention. However, it should not become a dependent relationship in which he is heartbroken without you. This broken heart can also bring on destructive behaviour as well as loss of appetite, depression and lack of interest in play and interaction. Canine behaviourists have been spending much time and energy to help owners better understand the significance of this stressful condition.

One thing you can do to minimise separation anxiety is to make your entrances and exits as low-key as possible. Do not give your dog a long drawn-out goodbye, and do not lavish him with hugs and kisses when you return. This is giving in to the attention that he craves, and it will only make him miss it more when you are away. Another thing you can try is to give your dog a treat when you leave; this

AGE OF ANXIETY
The number of dogs that suffer from separation anxiety is on the rise as more and more pet owners find themselves at work all day. New attention is being paid to this problem, which is especially hard to diagnose since it is only evident when the dog is alone. Research is currently being done to help educate dog owners about separation anxiety and how they can help minimise this problem in their dogs.

will not only keep him occupied and keep his mind off the fact that you have just left, but it will also help him associate your leaving with a pleasant experience.

You may have to accustom your dog to being left alone at intervals. Of course, when your dog starts whimpering as you approach the door, your first

I'M HOME!
Dogs left alone for varying lengths of time may often react wildly when their owners return. Sometimes they run, jump, bite, chew, tear things apart, wet themselves, gobble their food or behave in very undisciplined ways. If your dog behaves in this manner upon your return home, allow him to calm down before greeting him or he will consider your attention as a reward for his antics.

instinct will be to run to him and comfort him, but do not do it! Eventually he will adjust to your absence. His anxiety stems from being placed in an unfamiliar situation; by familiarising him with being alone, he will learn that he will survive. That is not to say you should purposely leave your dog home alone, but the dog needs to know that, while he can depend on you for his care, you do not have to be by his side 24 hours a day. Some behaviourists recommend tiring the dog out before you leave home—take him for a walk or engage in a game of fetch in the garden.

When the dog is alone in the house, he should be placed in his crate—another distinct advantage to crate training your dog. The crate should be placed in his familiar happy family area, where he normally sleeps and already feels comfortable, thereby making him feel more at ease when he is alone. Be sure to give the dog a special chew toy to enjoy while he settles into his crate.

SEXUAL BEHAVIOUR

Dogs exhibit certain sexual behaviours that may have influenced your choice of male or female when you first purchased your King Charles Spaniel. To a certain extent, spaying/neutering will eliminate these behaviours,

Fortunately for King Charles and their owners, the dogs' small size enables them to go along most anywhere.

but if you are purchasing a dog that you wish to breed from, you should be aware of what you will have to deal with throughout the dog's life.

Female dogs usually have two oestruses per year, with each season lasting about three weeks. These are the only times in which a female dog will mate, and she usually will not allow this until the second week of the cycle, although this varies from bitch to bitch. If not bred during the heat cycle, it is not uncommon for a bitch to experience a false pregnancy, in which her mammary glands swell and she exhibits

'X' MARKS THE SPOT

As a pack animal, your dog marks his territory as a way of letting any possible intruders know that this is his space and that he will defend his territory if necessary. Your dog marks by urinating because urine contains pheromones that allow other canines to identify him. While this behaviour seems like a nuisance, it speaks litres about your dog's mental health. Stable, well-trained dogs living in quiet, less populated areas may mark less frequently than less confident dogs inhabiting busy urban areas that attract many possible invaders. If your dog only marks in certain areas in your home, your bed or just the front door, these are the areas he feels obligated to defend. If your dog marks frequently, see your veterinary surgeon or an animal behaviourist.

maternal tendencies toward toys or other objects.

With male dogs, owners must be aware that whole dogs (dogs who are not neutered) have the natural inclination to mark their territory. Males mark their territory by spraying small amounts of urine as they lift their legs in a macho ritual. Marking can occur both outdoors in the garden and around the neighbourhood as well as indoors on furniture legs, curtains and the sofa. Such behaviour can be very frustrating for the owner; early training is strongly urged before the 'urge' strikes your dog. Neutering the male at an appropriate early age can solve this problem before it becomes an habit.

Other problems associated with males are wandering and mounting. Both of these habits, of course, belong to the unneutered dog, whose sexual drive leads him away from home in search of

MACHO GUSTO

Males, whether castrated or not, will mount almost anything: a pillow, your leg or, much to your horror, even your neighbour's leg. As with other types of inappropriate behaviour, the dog must be corrected while in the act, which for once is not difficult. Often he will not let go! While a puppy is experimenting with his very first urges, his owners feel he needs to 'sow his oats' and allow the pup to mount. As the pup grows into a full-size dog, with full-size urges, it becomes a nuisance and an embarrassment. Males always appear as if they are trying to 'save the race,' more determined and stronger than imaginable. While altering the dog at an appropriate age will limit the dog's desire, it usually does not remove it entirely.

the bitch in heat. Males will mount females in heat, as well as any other dog, male or female, that happens to catch their fancy. Other possible mounting partners include his owner, the furniture, guests to the home and strangers on the street. Discourage such behaviour early on.

Owners must further recognise that mounting is not merely a sexual expression but also one of dominance, seen in dogs and bitches alike. Be consistent and be persistent, and you will find that you can 'move mounters.'

CHEWING

The national canine pastime is chewing! Every dog loves to sink his 'canines' into a tasty bone, but sometimes that bone is in his owner's hand! Dogs need to chew to massage their gums, to make their new teeth feel better and to exercise their jaws. This is a natural behaviour that is deeply embedded in all things canine. Our role as owners is not to stop the dog's chewing, but rather to redirect it to positive, chew-worthy objects. Be an informed owner and purchase proper chew toys, like strong nylon bones, that will not splinter. Be sure that the objects are safe and durable, since your dog's safety is at risk. Again, the owner is responsible for ensuring a dog-proof environment.

The best answer is prevention; that is, put your shoes, handbags and other tasty objects in their proper places (out of the reach of the growing canine mouth). Direct puppies to their toys whenever you see them 'tasting' the furniture legs or the leg of your trousers. Make a loud

Chewing is most commonly associated with teething pups, but by no means does the urge to chew stop as the dog grows. Providing safe chew toys is of equal importance for puppies and adult dogs.

noise to attract the pup's attention and immediately escort him to his chew toy and engage him with the toy for at least four minutes, praising and encouraging him all the while. An array of safe, interesting chew toys will keep your dog's mind and teeth occupied, and distracted from chewing on things he shouldn't.

JUMPING UP

Jumping up is a dog's friendly way of saying hello! Some dog owners do not mind when their dog jumps up. The problem arises when guests come to the house and the dog greets them in the same manner—whether they like it or not! However friendly the greeting may be, the chances are that your visitors will not appreciate your dog's enthusiasm. The dog will not be able to distinguish upon whom he can jump and whom he cannot. Therefore, it is probably best to discourage this behaviour entirely.

Pick a command such as 'Off' (avoid using 'Down' since you will use that for the dog to lie down) and tell him 'Off' when he jumps up. Place him on the ground on all fours and have him sit, praising him the whole time. Always lavish him with praise and petting when he is in the sit position. In this way, you can give him a warm affectionate greeting, let him know that you are as excited to see him as he is

to see you and instil good manners at the same time!

DIGGING

Digging, which is seen as a destructive behaviour to humans, is actually quite a natural behaviour in dogs. Although terriers (the 'earth dogs') are most associated with digging, any dog's desire to dig can be irrepressible and most frustrating to his owners. The King Charles rarely exhibits a strong desire to dig, though every dog is an individual. When digging occurs

DOGS HAVE FEELINGS, TOO

You probably don't realise how much your dog notices the presence of a new person in your home as well as the loss of a familiar face. If someone new has moved in with you, your pet will need help adjusting. Have the person feed your dog or accompany the two of you on a walk. Also, make certain that your roommate is aware of the rules and routines that you have already set for your dog.

If you have just lost a longtime companion, there is a chance that you could end up with a case of 'leave me, leave my dog.' Dogs experience separation anxiety and depression, so watch for any changes in sleeping and eating habits and try to lavish a little extra love on your dog. It might make you feel better, too.

NO BUTTS ABOUT IT

Dogs get to know each other by sniffing each other's backsides. It seems that each dog has a telltale odour, probably created by the anal glands. It also distinguishes sex and signals when a female will be receptive to a male's attention. Some dogs snap at another dog's intrusion of their private parts.

he would be using may manifest itself in the form of little holes all over your garden and flower beds.

Perhaps your dog is digging as a reaction to boredom—it is somewhat similar to someone eating a whole bag of crisps in front of the TV—because they are there and there is nothing better to do! Basically, the answer is to provide the dog with adequate play and exercise so that his mind and paws are occupied, and so that he feels as if he is doing something useful.

Of course, digging is easiest to control if it is stopped as soon as possible, but it is often hard to catch a dog in the act. If your dog is a compulsive digger and is not easily distracted by other activities, you can designate an area on your property where he is allowed to dig. If you catch him digging in an off-limits area of the

in your garden, it is actually a normal behaviour redirected into something the dog can do in his everyday life. In the wild, a dog would be actively seeking food, making his own shelter, etc. He would be using his paws in a purposeful manner for his survival. Since you provide him with food and shelter, he has no need to use his paws for these purposes, and so the energy that

BELLY UP!

When two dogs are introduced, they will naturally establish who is dominant. This may involve one dog placing his front paws on the other's shoulders, or one dog rolling over and exposing his belly, thereby assuming a submissive status. If neither dog submits, they may fight until one has been pinned down. This behaviour can be upsetting for owners to watch, especially if your dog takes one look and throws himself on the ground. The biggest mistake you can make is to interfere, pulling on the leads and confusing the dogs. If you don't allow them to establish their pecking order, you undermine the pack mentality, which can cause your dog great stress. If you separate dogs in the middle of an encounter, the interference may incite them to attack each other viciously. Your best choice is to stay out of it!

BE NOT AFRAID

Just like humans, dogs can suffer from phobias including fear of thunder, fear of heights, fear of stairs or even fear of specific objects such as the swimming pool. To help your dog get over his fear, first determine what is causing the phobia. For example, your dog may be generalising by associating an accident that occurred on one set of stairs with every step he sees. You can try desensitisation training, which involves introducing the fear-trigger to your dog slowly, in a relaxed setting, and rewarding him when he remains calm. Most importantly, when your dog responds fearfully, do not coddle or try to soothe him, as this only makes him think that his fear is okay.

BARKING

King Charles Spaniels are quiet dogs, and few of them would ever be labelled 'yappy.' The King Charles tends to use his bark more purposefully and makes a suitable indoor watchdog. It is only when the barking becomes excessive, and when the excessive barking becomes a bad habit, that the behaviour needs to be modified. Excessive habitual barking, however, is a problem that should be corrected early on.

As your King Charles Spaniel grows up, you will be able to tell when his barking is purposeful and when it is for no reason. You will become able to distinguish your dog's different barks and their meanings. For example, the bark when someone comes to the door will be different from the bark when he is excited to see you. It is similar to a person's

garden, immediately take him to the approved area and praise him for digging there. Keep a close eye on him so that you can catch him in the act—that is the only way to make him understand what is permitted and what is not. If you take him to an hole he dug an hour ago and tell him 'No,' he will understand that you are not fond of holes, or dirt or flowers. If you catch him while he is stifle-deep in your tulips, that is when he will get your message.

HE'S PROTECTING YOU

Barking is your dog's way of protecting you. If he barks at a stranger walking past your house, a moving car or a fleeing cat, he is merely exercising his responsibility to protect his pack (YOU) and territory from a perceived intruder. Since the 'intruder' usually keeps going, the dog thinks his barking chased it away and he feels fulfilled. This behaviour leads your overly vocal friend to believe that he is the 'dog in charge.'

tone of voice, except that the dog has to rely totally on tone of voice because he does not have the benefit of using words. An incessant barker will be evident at an early age.

There are some things that encourage a dog to bark. For

example, if your dog barks non-stop for a few minutes and you give him a treat to quieten him, he believes that you are rewarding him for barking. He will associate barking with getting a treat and will keep doing it until he is rewarded. On the other hand, if you give him a command such as 'Quiet' and praise him after he has stopped barking for a few seconds, he will get the idea that being 'quiet' is what you want him to do.

FOOD STEALING
Is your dog devising ways of stealing food from your coffee table or cupboard? If so, you must answer the following questions: Is your King Charles Spaniel peckish, or is he 'constantly famished' like many dogs seem to be? Face it, some dogs are more food-motivated than others. They are totally obsessed by the smell of food and can only think of their next meal. Food stealing is terrific fun and always yields a great reward—FOOD, glorious food.

Your goal as an owner, therefore, is to be sensible about where food is placed in the home and to reprimand your dog whenever he is caught in the act of stealing. But remember, only reprimand your dog if you actually see him stealing, not later when the crime is discovered; that will be of no use at all and will only serve to confuse him.

BEGGING

Just like food stealing, begging is a favourite pastime of peckish puppies! It achieves that same lovely result—FOOD! Dogs quickly learn that their owners keep the 'good food' for themselves, and that we humans do not dine on dried food alone. Begging is a conditioned response related to a specific stimulus, time and place. The sounds of the kitchen, cans and bottles opening, crinkling bags, the smell of food in preparation, etc., will excite the dog, and soon the paws will be in the air!

Here is the solution to stopping this behaviour: Never give in to a beggar! You are rewarding the dog for sitting pretty, jumping up, whining and rubbing his nose into you by giving him food. By ignoring the dog, you will (eventually) force the behaviour into extinction. Note that the behaviour is likely to get worse before it disappears, so be sure there are not any 'softies' in the family who will give in to little 'Oliver' every time he whimpers, 'More, please.'

COPROPHAGIA

Faeces eating is, to humans, one of the most disgusting behaviours that their dogs could engage in; yet, to dogs, it is perfectly normal. It is hard for us to understand why a dog

> ### THE ORIGIN OF THE DINNER BELL
> The study of animal behaviour can be traced back to the 1800s and the renowned psychologist, Pavlov. When it was time for his dogs to eat, Pavlov would ring a bell, then feed the dogs. Pavlov soon discovered that the dogs learned to associate the bell with food and would drool at the sound of a bell. And you thought yours was the only dog obsessed with eating!

would want to eat his own faeces. He could be seeking certain nutrients that are missing from his diet, he could be just hungry or he could be attracted by the pleasing (to a dog) scent. While coprophagia most often refers to the dog's eating his own faeces, a dog may just as likely eat that of another animal as well if he comes across it. Dogs often find the stool of cats and horses

> ### SMILE!
> Dogs and humans may be the only animals that smile. A dog will imitate the smile on his owner's face when he greets a friend. The dog only smiles at his human friends; he never smiles at another dog or cat. Usually, a dog rolls up his lips and shows his teeth in a clenched mouth while rolling over onto his back, begging for a soft scratch.

more palatable than that of other dogs.

Vets have found that diets with low levels of digestibility, containing relatively low levels of fibre and high levels of starch, increase coprophagia. Therefore, high-fibre diets may decrease the likelihood of dogs' eating faeces. Both the consistency of the stool (how firm it feels in the dog's mouth) and the presence of undigested nutrients increase the likelihood. Once the dog develops diarrhoea from faeces eating, he will likely stop this distasteful habit.

To discourage this behaviour, first make sure that the food you are feeding your dog is nutritionally complete and that he is getting enough food. If changes in his diet do not seem to work, and no medical cause can be found, you will have to modify the behaviour through environmental control before it becomes an habit. The best way to prevent your dog from eating his stool is to make it unavailable—clean up after he eliminates and remove any stool from the garden. If it is not there, he cannot eat it.

Reprimanding for stool eating rarely impresses the dog. Vets recommend distracting the dog while he is in the act of stool eating. Coprophagia is seen most frequently in pups 6 to 12 months of age, and usually disappears around the dog's first birthday.

PHARMACEUTICAL FIX

There are two drugs specifically designed to treat mental problems in dogs. About 7 million dogs each year are destroyed because owners can no longer tolerate their dogs' behaviour, according to Nicholas Dodman, a specialist in animal behaviour at Tufts University in Massachusetts.

The first drug, Clomicalm, is prescribed for dogs suffering from separation anxiety, which is said to cause them to react when left alone by barking, chewing their owners' belongings, drooling copiously or defecating or urinating inside the home.

The second drug, Anipryl, is recommended for cognitive dysfunction syndrome or 'old dog syndrome,' a mental deterioration that comes with age. Such dogs often seem to forget that they were house-trained and where their food bowls are, and they may even fail to recognise their owners.

A tremendous human-animal bonding relationship is established with all dogs, particularly veteran dogs. This precious relationship deteriorates when the dog does not recognise his master. The drug can restore the bond and make veteran dogs feel more like their old selves.

INDEX

My King Charles Spaniel

PUT YOUR PUPPY'S FIRST PICTURE HERE

Dog's Name _____

Date _____ Photographer _____